Benji

Benji
MY STORY

Benji Marshall *with* Glenn Jackson

Hodder Moa

National Library of New Zealand Cataloguing-in-Publication Data
Marshall, Benji.
Benji : my story / by Benji Marshall with Glenn Jackson.
ISBN 978-1-86971-251-8
1. Marshall, Benji. 2. Rugby league football players—New Zealand—Biography.
1. Jackson, Glenn, 1976- II. Title.
796.3338092—dc 22

A Hodder Moa Book
Published in 2011 by Hachette New Zealand Ltd
4 Whetu Place, Mairangi Bay
Auckland, New Zealand
www.hachette.co.nz

Text © Benji Investments Pty Ltd
The moral rights of the author have been asserted.
Design and format © Hachette New Zealand Ltd 2011

All rights reserved. No part of this publication may be reproduced or transmitted in any form or by any means, electronic or mechanical, including photocopying, recording, or any information storage and retrieval system, without permission in writing from the publisher.

Designed and produced by Hachette New Zealand Ltd
Printed by Griffin Press, Australia

Front cover photo: Photosport
Back cover and back flap photos: Action Photographics

The paper this book is printed on is certified against the Forest Stewardship Council® Standards. Griffin Press holds FSC chain of custody certification SGS-COC-005088.
FSC promotes environmentally responsible, socially beneficial and economically viable management of the world's forests.

To the only man I called Dad, Michael Joseph Doherty, who treated me like his own son, and also to three women who touched my life and still inspire me to keep doing what I do, my grandmother Kahira Marshall, Aunty Mary and Aunty Judith. May you all rest in peace.

Contents

Foreword   11
Acknowledgements   15
Writer's note   19
Prologue   23

1	The First Steps	35
2	A Golden Age	53
3	Tiger Cub	69
4	A Pub Team	79
5	One Week of All Time	91
6	Grand Occasion	99
7	A Label	115
8	A Final Sling	123
9	God Defend Me	141
10	On Top of the World	155
11	Dad	169
12	Iron Maiden	183
13	Four Nations	193
14	A No-brainer	207
15	Boys Will Be Boys	225
16	The Next Step	239

About the Writer   253

Foreword

RARE ARE the moments, as a coach, when I can just sit back and enjoy a game of football. Benji Marshall gives me those moments. When he plays, I like to watch him play; really watch him. I will put the TV on and just watch him.

There haven't been many of those sorts of players during my career; Allan Langer, Andrew Johns, Darren Lockyer and Wally Lewis are some. Benji is up there with any of those players in terms of skill levels. If I get the chance to watch Benji play, I do. He has a different approach to the game. He equals anybody I've seen in terms of flair, and making something happen.

He is a remarkable talent, born out of living on the edge. That's the way he is. He was made to be a footballer; a bit unscripted, but he is what he is. That flick-pass in the grand final, that is what you get from those players. I am still in awe of that play; running one way, flat out, and throwing the ball in the other direction behind his back. That is simply uncoachable. Sometimes, he doesn't look like he knows what he's doing, and then all of a sudden he has beaten three guys and thrown a magnificent pass. But he knows he has to be part of the team. There is never a question mark about Benji being part of the team.

He is very conscious of his friends and his teammates. He has a concern and care about them that people don't always see.

And he's very smart, street smart. He listens, he is respectful and he takes advice. But, importantly, he makes his own decisions. He is his own man.

He is very conscious of his image in the game. He had a bit of a hiccup this year, but he certainly hasn't had a lot of problems with his profile. And that mustn't be easy for him. He's Benji Marshall. I've seen it; people want to touch Benji, they want him to sign autographs, they want him to pose for photographs. He only has to sneeze and someone will find fault. That puts a lot more pressure on him. He has always got to watch what he does, but he handles himself in a very classy manner, with a smile on his face.

I had my first significant dealing with him in the New Zealand camp for the 2008 World Cup. He was certainly an extroverted character, although that didn't come across immediately.

Prior to that I'd met Benji a couple of times, but never for any great length of time. We'd exchanged a few words here and there.

When I first saw him in camp, he was quite reserved. We subsequently built a very strong relationship, and he is someone I have always felt I could trust. He loves to laugh, and he loves to be leading the banter. He is fun to be around, and I think that helps him play the way he does.

I coached a guy named Allan Langer, and Benji's got a few of Alfie's traits — not all of them, mind you. But it was always important for Alfie to have fun and enjoy himself. If he wasn't laughing and enjoying himself, he wouldn't play well.

Benji remains the only person who has ever managed to get me into women's clothing. During the World Cup, in Newcastle, we decided to have a Melbourne Cup luncheon, and we all had to get dressed up in clothes that the players had picked up from a local St Vincent de Paul.

FOREWORD

We all picked names out of a hat. Whoever we picked out could choose what we wore. I got Benji, of course, and he dressed me up in drag. I had no alternative — a 58-year-old man dressed in drag! Benji was so proud of himself. I can still picture him giggling when he was looking at me.

Benji has a bit of cheekiness about him, but he is always conscious of other people's feelings. He doesn't target someone who can't handle it. There is no showmanship in Benji. He is who he is.

But most of all, I love the way he plays the game. I like the spirit he brings to his game, and the game. I really felt for him when he was going through injury after injury after injury. But in the last few years, we've seen him virtually injury-free. We've seen him become captain of New Zealand, which is something that he treasures and values. Every time he takes the field, he gives us enjoyment and excitement, and he makes it look like fun — he's entertaining himself and us. The game has benefited enormously from Benji being on the park. That has given us, and me, what we want. More of Benji Marshall.

Wayne Bennett
Sydney, July 2011

Acknowledgements

I WOULD like to thank the many people who have joined me on this path and helped me get to where I am today. A lot of my success, my discipline, and the way I am, is a tribute to the way I was raised as a child. Firstly, to my grandparents (Koro Toby and Nanny Kahira) for starting a very talented family, and for teaching us all the importance of family and love above all other things. To my uncles (Henry, Bruce, Sam, Phil, John, David, Bussy, Luke and Bensy), who taught me about what it takes to become a man and gave me the fighting spirit which helped me throughout my career. I thank you, particularly, because at some stage in my life you were all like fathers to me. To all of my aunties (Mary, Judith, Edith and Bethany), who taught me how to show my softer side, how to express myself, and for always keeping the male side of our family in check.

I would also like to thank, most importantly, the two women who had the biggest effect on my life growing up, my two mothers, Lydia and Annalie. I will forever be grateful for the support you have given me emotionally; and the way that you have both raised me and helped me become the man that I am today. You both go above and beyond, no matter what.

To Lydia: to have me at the age you did, and for the amount of things we have been through and the adversity we have overcome, I am truly grateful. It is no fluke that I got through all the tough times the way I did when I look back and see you as a 16-year-old single mother.

To Annalie, thank you for helping out Lydia when she was younger — and then accepting me as your own. From as far back as I can remember, I have considered you my mum, and it will always be that way.

A big thank you to the entire Doherty family for accepting me as one of your own and making me feel like family. To Paula, Nicola and Michelle, you are the older sisters I never would have had if I wasn't welcomed into the family. To Andrew and Troy, a lot of the skills I learnt, from golf to tennis to kicking the ball around to drinking beer, were all things I learnt from you two (especially the drinking games). Thank you for being big brothers, especially Andrew for music, tennis and golf, and Troy for always making me cry.

To my two little brothers, Jordan and Jeremy, I thank you for giving me the motivation to want to be something great. Everything I do, I try to do for you two.

A special thank you to all my cousins for the time we spent together growing up, getting in trouble, getting hidings together and for all the years we used to lose to the adults at Christmas in all the games. But now the roles have reversed and they are too scared to play us any more. (Marshall Mob Hard!)

To Uncle Bens, you have been my rock throughout my whole life, always there no matter what. Whenever I felt in trouble or needed someone to talk to, you were there. To me, you are like my father, and I will always be in debt to you. If it wasn't for you, I would not have met the Dohertys. Thank you also to Aunty Michelle; you must be the first aunty/sister in the world. Thanks for being there for me with Uncle Bens. Uncle, I am

ACKNOWLEDGEMENTS

proud to have been named after you. You are the real and first Benjamin Marshall.

Last but not least from my family, I would like to thank (even though you are not here) the only man I called Dad (Mick). You were the nicest person I have ever come across and the reason I found my way a lot of the time when I was lost. You will be forever missed. Rest in peace, Dad.

Thank you very much to Martin and Barbara Tauber for accepting me into your home and for managing my career. Martin, if it wasn't for you, I wouldn't be where I am today. You keep me grounded and are the reason I am where I am financially — not to mention the reason I know so much about red wine.

To all the people I lived with along my journey: Aunty Beth and Uncle Rob, Aunty Mary, Aunty Judith, Uncle Bruce, Uncle Phil, Paris and Tracy Kingi, Uncle Chiefy and Aunty Janet, the Poland family, the Teague family, The Dayberg-Muir family, the Moonah Crew, Jason Stanton, Steve and Karen Lavers, Dean and Nathan Lavers, Bo Dela Cruz, Jai Chan, Paul Whatuira, Taniela Tuiaki, Bronson Harrison, Aunty Chris and the Henry Street Crew, Harlen, Gus, Moltz and Woody. Thank you all.

To all my mates on the Gold Coast for helping me through, in particular from Keebra Park: Harley, Nigel, Ms Anne Pike, Mr Peter Craig, Mr Greg Lenton, Mrs Fran Jones, Woolfey and Kurt.

Also to Kane George, Shannon Eckstein, The Mock aka Matt Anderson and Drummy — thanks for having my back all those years before I became who I am and even more for still being there now.

To all the players and staff of the Wests Tigers, thank you for your support throughout my time at the club. To all the players and staff, past and present, from the NZRL, thank you too. To the Western Suburbs touch football club crew. And to all the people who have coached me throughout my life, thank you.

To all my mates, from the ones I made growing up to the friends I have now, thank you for everything we have been through and all your support throughout my life. I could name you all, but there are too many and we would run out of pages.

Lastly, I would like to thank everyone involved in making this book happen, to Warren Adler and Matthew Kelly at Hachette, and especially Glenn Jackson and your family, for the tireless hours you spent chasing me and the hours of your own time to put this all together. It is exactly how I wanted my life explained, and for that I thank you.

Benjamin Quentin Marshall
Sydney, July 2011

Writer's note

DON'T JUDGE a book by its cover. We are constantly told this. So consider this one. On it, you will see a confident and brash young man, which is what Benji Marshall is. But it is also what he isn't.

On the field, he is rarely not a picture of confidence: all energy, effervescence and verve. But what became clear during the process of researching Marshall's life and career so far is that, ever the performer, he is equally adept at putting on a show off the field as on it.

Before I came across Benji Marshall, I had been told that he was cocky. It was difficult to argue that he wasn't. By the time I met him for the first time, I was convinced he was arrogant. I had the audacity to miss a portion of his impromptu press conference after he starred for the Tigers and he gave me a little serve for asking whether he'd go over old ground with me again. He did so, I believe, to keep up appearances; to show me who was boss but also to show everyone else. He still gave that interview. There is very little difference between precocious and precious and I erred in mistaking one for the other.

He is a hard nut to crack, but when you do there is a soft centre. For all the performances he is most proud of — the flick pass in the grand final of 2005, setting up the winning try in the World Cup final of 2008, the Golden Boot of 2010 and his club's Iron Man award of the same year — I sense that the one he considers on top of them all is his eulogy to his father. I make no error in referring to Mick Doherty as his father. That is how Benji sees him. He never knew his paternal father, but he had many men in his life who made up for it. I met many of them during a family reunion near Wellington, in early 2010; it is easy to see where Benji gets his fighting spirit. They are tough men.

The side of Benji that was more surprising was the tender one. To hear him speak so emotionally about his dad, showing a soft heart underneath his battered and scarred skin, was my highlight of this process. Annalie Doherty, Mick's wife, who would become Benji's second mother, told me one of her regrets was that Mick could not contribute to his son's autobiography. But it is so clear that he has; the man had more impact and influence on Benji Marshall than most. He still got to see the talent that he nurtured on his Whakatane farm flourish. It has been some career to this point.

When, as a schoolkid, Benji Marshall bounced into an NRL career, it was clear he was different. He had a step like no other. If South African cricketer Paul Adams's bowling action was described as 'frog in a blender', then Benji's stepping style is a frog trying to avoid the blender. All exaggerated hop, skip and mid-air shimmy.

Through his career, many have been as intrigued by Benji off the field as they have on it, which clearly frustrates him greatly. This book has coincided with one of his most difficult years off the field, and I thank him for putting his time and his heart into documenting his life.

The story which sums Benji Marshall up best is the one which involves a fast food restaurant. But it's not the one you're thinking of. The night before the grand final of '05, Marshall

WRITER'S NOTE

attended a twenty-first birthday of a friend, before heading back to the home of Dene Halatau's family with a bagful of McDonald's burgers and fries. How a 20-year-old, about to play in the biggest game of his life, can fill his stomach with that instead of nerves beggars belief. Benji should not be defined by what happens at a fast food restaurant — and yet he should be.

This book would not have happened without the help of many people. Thanks especially to Benji's manager Martin Tauber, who has been guiding 'the boy', as he calls him, since he made his first-grade debut and, doing much of his work behind the scenes, probably does not get enough thanks in these pages. A debt of gratitude also to Warren Adler and Matthew Kelly, from the New Zealand and Australian arms of publisher Hachette, for their enthusiasm and guidance, as well as Janette Doolan, who worked tirelessly to transcribe hours of interviews. Others to have contributed greatly are, in no particular order, Tim Sheens, Wayne Bennett, Phil Gould, Scott Prince, Stephen Humphreys and Greg Lenton. Thanks also to the *Sydney Morning Herald*'s chief sports editor, Ian Fuge, and sports editor Ben Coady for allowing me to moonlight with a Marshall, as well as my colleagues Brad Walter, Greg Prichard and Chris Barrett, whose talents ensured I could do so without neglecting my daily round. And Benji's family, of course: mothers Lydia and Annalie, and his uncle Bensy, who casts an imposing and so important shadow over the man who was named after him. And my family: wife Chantal and children Kaelan and Sassika, who had to ride the ups and downs of Benji's career in order for me to write them.

This autobiography is by no means meant to be definitive. The full stop at the bottom of the final page will not be the end. Benji Marshall is 26 years old, possibly only just past the halfway point of his career.

But Benji has been through more in his years thus far than many would see in a long career. He has won a premiership and a World Cup and has undergone four shoulder reconstructions; any one of those injuries could have made this an end-of-career autobiography rather than a mid-career one. He went through all that before he was 23. The best may yet be to come. This is, truly, the first step. The brash boy from Whakatane, New Zealand, to whom this story belongs, will believe that to be the case. He can only hope the hardest has passed him. What we can be sure of is that whatever is left will be entertaining.

Glenn Jackson
Sydney, July 2011

Prologue

THE SIZE of the needle worried me more than the tip of it. It looked longer than my forearm. It was called a block, because it blocked out the pain, I guessed, and I would have four of these needles over time, each one worse than the last. Not in terms of physical pain, mind you. I never actually felt the point of that needle in the crook of my neck. It was deemed so painful that I had to be given a general anaesthetic first, so that it could be administered; an anaesthetic for an anaesthetic. The 'block' was the biggest needle I'd seen in my life but, really, it was the least of my worries.

In my family, I am looked up to as someone who is strong, and who could handle setbacks. But through the injuries and surgeries that I went through, I cried many times; I'd sit in my room, alone and broken. I didn't want any of my family to think that I was weak. But I was feeling weak, mentally weak. I have all the fighting qualities in me to never give up, but there were stages when the drain on me was just so heavy that I wanted to.

The worst moments? The 2007 shoulder injury, my fourth and last, was the most difficult to get through. But there were awful experiences through all of my injuries. Some of them were just surreal. On one occasion, I drove to the doctor's surgery in someone else's car, with tinted windows, to avoid and evade the eyes behind the television cameras. I asked my teammate, Jamahl Lolesi, to drive my car and park it up the road — the cameras would run to the car and realise it was Jamahl, and then I'd sneak into the surgery.

I couldn't handle the scrutiny for a long time. I couldn't handle the pressure I was being put under, and I didn't like the way I was being perceived. Through that period, I did a lot of drinking. It was my way of relaxing. I couldn't play so I'd go out on weekends and get drunk, to release a lot of tension.

Looking back, I don't know how I got through it, and to sit here now, after winning the World Cup, a Four Nations, and the Golden Boot since then, I think: 'How did I get to here?' I never take anything for granted any more. From one end of the scale, being on top of the world in 2005 after winning the premiership, to the other end, almost quitting, being in a place that is so dark and dull. My shoulders were ticking time bombs for a long period. *Tick, tick, tick.* I never knew when they were going to go on me. And I never knew whether the next tackle was going to mean the end of my career. It was difficult trying to play at my best every week, when in the snap of a finger, or a shoulder joint, I could be finished.

I DON'T know why all those problems started, but I do know when and where. It wasn't early, and it wasn't in New Zealand. I had hardly any injury problems when I was younger. I broke my right collarbone when I was 14 and still at high school, while playing rugby union. But that was the extent of my troubles as a kid.

My shoulders were always quite flexible. I've had surgeons tell me I have loose shoulders — although they're fairly tight

PROLOGUE

now after all the reconstructions I've had on them. I believe my problems may be genetic. Many of my family members had the same problems. Cousins, brothers . . . many of them have had shoulder issues.

My own problems began in 2004. My coach, Tim Sheens, started to play me in the centres at the start of that year. I played three games there, and I wasn't enjoying it at all. I told him I wanted to play five-eighth. He said, 'We'll give you a couple of weeks at centre. I've done it with Laurie Daley.' I have heard that so many times. *I did it with Laurie Daley.* I think of it as the old Laurie Daley speech. I've heard it a thousand times — I still hear it. 'We can play that kid at centre, I did it with Laurie Daley — actually, I did it with you!' That's a new one now. Eventually, Tim moved me back to five-eighth. I felt like I was killing it.

Then, against the Cowboys, in my eleventh game of the year, it all changed. I sprinted out of the line from a drop-out, trying to prove I was tough, to hit the biggest man on the field in their prop Paul Rauhihi. I rushed ahead of everyone else, I put my head down, and he changed direction. Instead of running away from me, he ran straight at me. I was on my own, and thinking that I'd smash him — quite stupidly given I was about 77 kg — and I threw everything at him. Only problem was, he threw everything at me as well. When he did hit me, my left shoulder popped out of the socket. I heard the pop, but what I felt first was just an awkward feeling more than anything else. Numb, too. Everywhere. It was as if I'd become deaf — I couldn't hear anyone around me. All I could think about was my shoulder. The game just carried on, and I just stood there. My teammates, not realising what had happened, were yelling at me to get back in the line to defend. I tried to pull my arm, then the trainer came on and — click — popped it back into place.

I hurried straight off into the dressing room, but, as I recall, I wasn't really worried at all. I didn't realise the significance of it. It was just a dislocated shoulder to me. I was young and naive, I guess.

I WAS a little claustrophobic back then, which made my first MRI scan a very uncomfortable experience. I was lying in this machine, in a clinic in Pennant Hills, and I felt like my head was being squashed. It was a very strange sensation. I was given a button I could push if I didn't feel comfortable, a panic button, and it didn't take long for me to use it. I panicked very quickly, and the man who was operating it had to pull me out and calm me down. He told me the easiest way to get through it was just to close my eyes — and not open them at all. I never did open them, in all the subsequent shoulder scans I had.

The Wests Tigers doctor, Donald Kuah, explained to me that I could try to rehabilitate the shoulder for six weeks, strengthen it and play again relatively quickly. Or I could have surgery and miss the rest of the season. There was only one option for a young bloke wanting to make his mark.

I didn't know any better then. Looking back, if I knew what I know now, I probably would have just opted for the immediate surgery. But it was my first proper year in first grade — I'd only played a handful of matches the year before — and we were going quite well as a team. I wanted to be a part of it. So I decided to rehab it, doing physio every day and strengthening exercises with a Thera-Band, a stretch strap. I did that for 45 minutes at a time, three or four times a day, when I wasn't at training. When I was at training, I did it for an hour before training and then again after it — while my teammates trained I ran.

PROLOGUE

So I played on, for a while at least. I felt good after four weeks, and returned earlier than I was supposed to. I played a part in the first three-match winning streak in the club's history, but in my fourth game back I dislocated the same shoulder in Melbourne, trying to tackle Storm centre Steve Bell. He scooted from dummy-half; I was at marker and I slipped over, his weight came down on my shoulder and it popped straight out again.

Surgery was the only option. It was too weak. My season, what was meant to be my first full one, was over.

I HATE the smell of hospitals. Nothing against this one, the Mater at Crows Nest; I hate all of them. I hate the waiting rooms. It's the process I hate, too; nothing to eat or drink after a certain time. I didn't know what to expect the first time. I'd never had surgery before and it was quite daunting.

The nurse shaved my armpit, which was weird, and then drew an arrow in thick black Texta pen on my shoulder, so the surgeon knew which one was being operated on. I had to tell them my name, and what I was having done. An open left-shoulder reconstruction. I signed a form.

Then came the 'block'. I remember the name of the man who gave it to me, Colin Norgate, the anaesthetist. He has been there every time I have had my shoulders operated on. He is a good bloke. He asked me about footy and other things. Then he said to me, 'I'm going to have to knock you out for a little while, but you'll come to soon. Then when you're on the operating table you'll get the full load.' I asked him why. 'You don't want to know,' he said. 'Tell me,' I reasoned. Then he showed me the block needle, which was about to be inserted in my neck. I was petrified of it. Then he just said, 'Ta-ta.'

I woke up and I couldn't feel my mouth. My tongue was numb. The anaesthetic, given through my hand, just felt so cold. Even now, that feeling gives me shivers. I know it too well. You get pins and needles in your head, and then nothing. I woke up in a room by myself, frightened and disorientated. I wondered if I'd had the surgery. I could see some saloon doors, with circular windows on each of them. I could just see the top of the surgeon's head — he must have been already working on someone. I was so scared, because I didn't know what had happened. So I started singing, thinking that someone would hear me. But because my mouth was so numb, I couldn't sing properly. One of the nurses came in, looked at me, and I kept trying to sing. She just laughed.

I felt like I was a little kid. I could have been awake for only 10 minutes, but it felt like five hours. I was pushed into the operating theatre, and I remember someone being still on the operating table. They left me to the side, and they kept working. And all of a sudden I'm asleep again. I woke up again as they were lifting me onto the table. *Three, two, one.*

The surgeon, Des Bokor, spoke to me for a while, and then he said: 'You'll be right, mate. We'll see you later.' He made me count backwards from 10. All I remember was '10'. I was out again.

I woke up in the recovery room. It felt like waking up in somebody else's house, not knowing where you are. When you fall asleep you're in the theatre but when you come round you're in another room. It felt pretty scary at the time. There were five other beds around me, people with tubes up their noses lying on them.

The tube was quickly taken out of mine; it had extended right down my throat. I was so thirsty, but I couldn't tell the nurse. It was a horrible feeling. I couldn't speak because everything was so numb. I couldn't lift my arm up, so I tried to communicate

PROLOGUE

with my toes. She grabbed an ice cube and put it in my mouth. It was just about the best feeling I've had. I was so thirsty, so dehydrated, and I could just taste hospital tubes. That awful sterilised taste.

The nurses checked my blood pressure every few minutes, and whether I had any feeling in my hands. They kept playing with my fingers, but I couldn't feel anything. When I started feeling better, they took me to my room.

I only found out later — I don't actually remember doing it myself — but when I got back to my room I started ringing all these people and telling them the operation was a success. They all said I sounded drunk.

By then I was so hungry. I was given a quarter of a ham and cheese sandwich, and another with egg. Both triangles had no crust. The nurse warned me not to eat too much, because of the nausea. So I ate both those sandwiches, and ordered a pizza. It was almost midnight, and there I was, ringing Domino's Pizza, ordering two pizzas. All I can say is, the nurse was spot on. I ate one piece of pizza, and threw it all back up.

I didn't know at the time, but I had a drain attached to me for the excess blood and whatever else; a tube pinned to my shoulder via my armpit and then pegged to the bed, running through to a disposable bag. If I needed to go to the toilet, I was meant to either go in the bedpan, or the nurse would have to help me to the toilet. I didn't know this, so I just tried to get up myself. When I moved, the drain pulled a touch out of my shoulder. The pain was awful.

IT WAS incredibly difficult to sleep. I had ice on my shoulder, which needed to be changed regularly. The nurse checked my blood pressure hourly. I spent most of the night staring at the ceiling.

In the morning, my manager, Martin Tauber, who lived around the corner, brought me two bacon and egg rolls. By then I could eat without being sick. I had those two and then asked for two more. I hadn't eaten properly for almost two days.

I thought I'd be in hospital for at least three days, but the next thing I knew I was out. Because Martin lived so close, I stayed with him for a few days. At the time I was living with a friend, my touch football teammate Jason Stanton, at Belfield, and it was too much of a hassle to get there. I didn't have any family in the country, but Martin looked after me well.

I was still in high spirits. *First major injury. Everyone gets hurt at some point in time.* I had two weeks in New Zealand, back at home with my family. But then I was straight back into rehab.

Few people understand how much hard work goes into recovering from an injury. In the beginning, it was three hours a day of exercises — three lots of one-hour routines. At the start it was all about improving my range of movement. But it was monotonous; the same exercises every day.

I was in a sling for two months before the surgeon pulled the stitches out. The worst thing was trying to shower — I couldn't wash under my armpit. It would stink, but there was nothing I could do about it, because I couldn't lift my arm up. I was always trying to spray deodorant to at least try to prevent some of the body odour.

Eventually, I was able to run, but not with the team. That was the worst part of it, the feeling of being left out. It still is the worst part. You either have to train by yourself or with other injured players. Much of the time I only had Andrew Leeds, the club physiotherapist, for company. That year, I was the only player who missed a full season, and I felt like a bit of an outcast. But, eventually, I would feel strong. I was back into training and back with the boys. I'd done all the hard work, and I thought it would be my first, and only, major injury. Yeah, right.

I DESPISE the term 'injury prone'. Only people who have been given that label know what it's like. I returned to footy in a trial in 2005 against an Italian combination in Ulladulla, and I felt strong. I was tackling hard, putting some shots on and feeling confident; maybe a little overconfident. With about five minutes remaining, one of their big front-rowers hit the ball up; I had to dive to tackle him, but as I did his knee hit the front of my right shoulder, and pushed it out of its socket.

I didn't realise what had happened until I returned to the defensive line and looked at my shoulder, noticing my arm was no longer where it was meant to be. If I tried to hold my right arm out in front of me, parallel to the ground, it would instead point about 45 degrees to my right.

And it was stuck there. The last time, the trainer put it back in place quickly, but it was much harder to do on this occasion. I put my hand up, my other one, the medical staff realised what had happened, and I left the field.

This was the year the jerseys started to get a lot tighter: skin-tight. I was yelling at anyone who'd listen to cut the damn thing. But they wouldn't. So I had to manoeuvre out of it, with my shoulder still dislocated.

Steve Noyce, the Tigers chief executive at the time, had a consoling hand on my left shoulder, which had been my bad one but which was now my good one. Dr Kuah told someone to hold me from behind, bear-hugging me under my armpits to hold my body still, and he pulled my arm away from me. That pain was up there with the worst I've felt. After he popped it back in, however, it felt much better. For about 15 minutes, anyway.

I started crying. I couldn't help myself. The coach didn't even make a speech after the game. The doctor was trying to talk to me out the back of the old sheds at the local footy oval. There were people looking at me, and I was shattered. I went to walk away and he grabbed my good arm. I pushed him away. I apologised to him later, but at the time I was so angry and frustrated I couldn't help it. I'd done so much hard work to return to the field, and then in a split second I was back to square one.

We had to do a promo in the local pub, and I just didn't want to be there. The doc told me to see him at his office on the Monday to discuss the options. He couldn't really give me an indication. It's very difficult knowing you're injured but not knowing how serious the damage is.

I had an MRI scan (same story; eyes closed to mask the claustrophobia), and he said it was pretty bad, that I'd need surgery again. But he gave me the same options as he had done the previous year: have surgery immediately or rehab it for six weeks and try to push through the season. There was about a 90 percent chance I would get through the season if I went with the second option. I took the gamble again, and I ended up playing every game except the first round. I wore a shoulder brace for the remainder of it, hoping that it would prevent my shoulder from being put in a vulnerable position. That made it very difficult to pass, as well as catch. I couldn't reach up high to catch. My shoulder was strapped every game, and I had physio on it every week.

There were occasions when it hurt so much I needed a

PROLOGUE

painkilling injection just so I could get through the game. And it was just so loose. I could actually feel how loose it was. That made me tentative to make tackles and it made me change my technique, because I was scared to put my arm out or dive into tackles. I was very nervy about dislocating it again.

But I wanted to get through the season. Tim started defending me on the wing; that probably saved me from injuring it again. Teams couldn't target me on the wing, and they wouldn't change their game plans to get to me.

The safe decision would have been getting the surgery done straight away. I didn't know any better. I just wanted to play. I certainly don't regret my decision, but part of me looks back and wonders if I would have had so many problems later if I'd had surgery at the start of 2005, rather than rolling the dice. It was the right decision for everything bar my long-term health.

If I had gone under the knife straight away, maybe it would have been the end of my shoulder troubles, but I wouldn't have a premiership. People often talk about the highs and lows of professional sport. I'm reminded of the extremes every time I look in the mirror, at a premiership tattoo on my left bicep and a surgery scar just a few inches above it. The best and worst of rugby league.

Chapter 1

The First Steps

'IF YOU can't handle it, piss off home.' If I could pick eight defining words, I would choose those ones. I heard them when I was about 10 years old, playing touch football at the local park in Whakatane, just over the neighbour's back fence, with my uncles and cousins.

My uncles, a competitive bunch, always used to try to rough me and my cousins up. Instead of a touch they would throw in something closer to a punch, or just push me over. I was usually the youngest there by at least five years, playing against men, mean ones, too. They never went soft on me. On the contrary, on this day, I copped three or four heavy-handed touches, before my Uncle Phil pushed me so hard that I felt like I'd broken a bone. I started crying, and he offered the words that have followed me ever since. 'You wanna play with the big boys, that's what happens. If you can't handle it, piss off home.'

So I did. I swore at him and said, 'I'm going home.' I sprinted home, with Uncle Phil chasing me part of the way. I sat at home crying under my pillow, thinking someone was going to feel sorry for me and come home. But no one came. After five minutes, I realised no one was going to. So I thought to myself, 'I'm going to go back and I'm going to show them.'

I walked back, still wiping the tears from my eyes and the snot from my nose. Uncle Phil said to me: 'Are you ready to play with the big boys?' I said: 'Yeah, let's go.' And they all gave me a hug or a tap on the shoulder.

I honestly believe that day at the local park helped me through the injuries I would suffer many years later. I think it was the most significant moment of my early life, at least when it comes to an influence on my sporting career. I learnt a lot about toughness, and bouncing back. I gave up and went home, but then I wanted to fight back. I thought to myself, 'I'm not going to let you beat me this time.' That sort of attitude would later serve me well.

This book details my life story and I make no apologies for penning it now. In it I cry many times, not just because of a push by an uncle. I have felt like giving in on many occasions, not least after two of four shoulder reconstructions, with my world collapsing around me. I would not wish some of it on anyone. Was it worth it? Of course it was.

I WAS born a breech baby and, would you believe, blond. I have always believed my talent to step people came partly because I arrived feet first. I cannot explain what went on at the other end. I was blond until I was seven or eight years old. Maybe the milkman was blond. It was truly weird.

My family was hardly a nuclear one, although it was certainly combustible. I was born and raised in Whakatane, a smallish coastal town in the eastern Bay of Plenty in New Zealand. It was my home for my entire childhood bar a brief period, six months or so at age 10, when I lived in Wellington. My mother, Lydia, was 16 when she gave birth to me. My father was someone I did not know. Later, I would not care to.

THE FIRST STEPS

Named Benjamin Quentin, nicknamed Benj (I would not be known as Benji until my move to the Gold Coast — I think it was that Australian habit of just putting an 'i' or a 'y' on the end of a name), I was often juggled between my grandmother, my cousins or my uncles, while my mum worked.

My mum had other responsibilities. My grandmother, Kahira, died when I was almost three. My mum had looked after her as she battled breast cancer. After she died, I remember being walked out of the house, out to the old letterbox. I was taken away from the house, where much of the Marshall family had gathered. I really don't know why it is that particular memory that sticks in my mind, but I do remember knowing that something bad had happened. The day she died is still a vivid memory, perhaps my first. For anything earlier, I will have to rely on my family to piece together my first years. Thankfully, family is something I was never short on. Many people played a role in my upbringing.

I HAD uncles who I regarded as fathers and many other people who fed and housed me. Most of my family lived in Whakatane, and I never needed to walk far to find an open door or a bed to sleep on.

The house I would first call home was built by my grandfather, Toby, and is still in the family to this day. My grandfather was a jack of all trades. We used to have the most beautiful gardens, with fruit trees that he'd planted. He did everything when it came to that house. Fixed everything.

The house had four bedrooms, which sounds a lot but was still far too small for my grandparents, who had 14 children. When a new baby arrived, sometimes the oldest would be forced to move out. There would sometimes be three or four to a room, two sharing single mattresses. A few of my uncles were living on the street by the time they were eight or nine, trying to fend for themselves, eating oranges or lemons from the neighbours' trees.

Thankfully, by the time I arrived, the house was far less crowded.

I HAVE always been something of a mummy's boy. I slept in my mother's bed until I was about 10. I used to be scared of the dark, and I felt safe next to her. I also have all the admiration in the world, and the utmost respect, for her; trying to raise me while also looking after her own mother. Mum was always ringing me, always worried about me. But I was fairly independent at a young age. I had to grow up long before I was meant to. By age eight, I could stay at home by myself for the weekend. That's just how it was. I was used to it.

I was also used to not having a father, at least in the strictest sense of the word. You don't miss what you don't know.

I do not know my paternal father's name. If I saw him in the street, I would not recognise him. That does not bother me, and I do not want to know him now. He has been out of my life for 26 years. Just because I have made something of it would not give him the right to walk back into it now.

I never felt like I wanted to know him. I do recall asking my mother about him, but the conversation didn't turn out too well, so I didn't ask again.

It never really fazed me. It made bringing me up, I guess, harder for my mother, but my life has turned out this way because of everything that has happened, including not knowing my father. Maybe it helped me. I had so many fathers growing up, I never felt that I did not have a dad; my uncles, who all treated me

THE FIRST STEPS

like their son — Bensy, Bussy (James), Luke, Phil, David, Henry, even Sam, John and Bruce, who lived in Wellington. There was also my foster father, Mick. At no stage did I ever feel like I was missing something.

The hardest moments were at school, when the other kids would ask, 'What does your dad do?' I always told them what Mick did. I had a dad. He was a farmer.

YOU COULD call me a wanderer. I lived with my Uncle Phil for a few years, my Aunty Bethany, who lived in the house in front of my grandfather's with Uncle Robert, and on and off, with my aunties Mary and Judith, too. I always wanted to hang out with my cousins. On holidays in Wellington, Uncle John would take me under his wing. I'd stay with my Uncle Luke, too. Everyone understood that my mum was young, and no one complained. They would give me their own money, paying for me to be able to do things with their own kids.

My Uncle Bensy was the closest thing I had to a father early on. He is still a father figure to this day. When I was at school, he would always swing by and give me money for lunch. He didn't have a lot of money, but he'd always find a $5 note to give me.

He was married when he was 18, and he would take me out to the home of his parents-in-law, Annalie and Michael Doherty, who lived about two kilometres outside town. They mentioned to my mother that they could adopt me, or at least help to look after me.

My mother never liked the idea of adopting me out, but she quite liked the prospect of them helping out. Ever since I can remember really, I have been living with my mum, who gave birth to me, and the couple who I also call Mum and Dad. I would ring Mick and Annalie and ask to go to their house for the afternoon, to play on the tennis court, the pool or on the trampoline. Then it became weekends. The only downside to that was the fact that I'd have to go to church on weekends. Dad would get us to church by bribing us with wine gums and burger rings. We'd always stop at the store in town on the way home from church. I got a bit smarter later on. I would tell Dad I didn't feel well, but I still asked for some wine gums.

Dad could never say no to me. Mum would tell me I couldn't have any more chocolate biscuits from the pantry so I'd instead ask Dad. 'Yeah, boy, help yourself.' The first thing Dad would do when he came inside after work was make a coffee or a tea. I'd see Mum in the sunroom, and I'd ask him for a biscuit. He'd bring the entire container out for me. 'You eat all the biscuits?' Mum would ask. 'Dad said I could,' I'd reply. She would already know that.

When I introduced them, I always said 'Mum and Dad'. I don't remember calling them anything else. I was never embarrassed to do so because that's what they were. Some people would look at us as if we were a bit strange. They looked a bit older than my parents should. I'd have to explain the story to them. Some people just assumed they were my grandparents. Not many people knew about Mick and Annalie when I was younger. That changed when I got a bit older, and people started to understand.

They were two different worlds. I spoke Maori a lot of the time with my blood family. My uncles and grandfather were fluent.

We never had much money. I used to have Weet-Bix for breakfast, lunch and dinner sometimes. But not with milk. That was a luxury. For flavour, I used to add butter and hot water. I took tomato sauce sandwiches to school. It was either that or Devon luncheon — I preferred tomato sauce sandwiches.

THE FIRST STEPS

Mick and Annalie were, by comparison, financially stable. They always had lollies and biscuits, and I was spoilt there. I would look forward to diving into the biscuit jar, and enjoying things I couldn't have at my other home. Mum had a birthday cake book, and I could pick any cake I wanted.

Mick was a big influence. I spent half my life with him. He never put me down but he told me where I could improve. And he'd always tell me I played well. 'Geez, you played good today, boy,' he'd say, even when I hadn't. He was very encouraging, and never had a bad word to say about anyone. I never heard him swear once. He and Annalie went to church every Sunday.

Sport was still important. I'd muck around with Troy and Andrew, their two boys, practising goal-kicking using the posts that they'd put up in the paddock. I was like Troy's shadow. Wherever he was, I'd be following. 'I'll give you two bucks if you catch this,' he'd say, throwing me the ball. Then I'd catch it. 'Double or nothing,' he'd say. If I took too much money off him, he'd throw one to me that was impossible to catch. He taught me a lot of skills.

They had plenty of land to make use of. Mick used to have cattle, selling the beef, but he also farmed maize. He'd plant it, fertilise the ground, harvest it, then load it into the trucks so it could be dried. I used to love helping him out, playing around in the tractors. He taught me how to drive in the paddock, with one of the trucks, which I crashed once. Mick used to sit me on his lap. He would put the truck in gear and just let it roll. So when he was feeding out hay to the cattle, all I had to do was steer, because the truck was in first gear.

Later, he showed me how to drive manually, using the clutch. When I was about nine, he told me to head through the gate; instead of steering wider, I tried to cut the corner and scraped the whole side of his favourite truck on the fence. I slammed the brakes on and he almost fell off the back of the truck.

I helped Mick whenever I stayed there. He'd say, 'Jump in the back of the truck and we'll go for a ride.' We'd check the cattle, and if any of them were out, we'd round them up and get them back in the paddock. We'd feed them. We'd find firewood. They are some of my favourite memories.

IT WAS a different life there. But I don't feel that one life was better than the other. I consider myself fortunate that I experienced the harder side of life and a more prosperous one. My lives, and families, crossed on occasions, mainly for Christmas. I'd spend Christmas Day with the Marshall family first, and then we'd drive out to Mick and Annalie's. We'd have Christmas there, too. Everyone would come together on my birthday also.

I was always spoilt in other ways at my other home, or homes. With the Marshall family, I was always playing sports, out as a family playing touch football or basketball. Everything we did was done as a family, even stealing the neighbour's grapefruit. No one ever complained or cried over no milk. If we did complain, we'd get a hiding.

My uncles were good at dishing out that particular form of tough love. I didn't like it then, but I don't resent it for a second. We never locked our house, because if anyone broke in they knew they'd have to deal with the Marshalls, most of whom have black belts in some form of martial arts.

Many of them were involved in their own martial arts group, nicknamed ROA. It stood for Rangataua o Aotearoa. John was one of the top dogs, but Luke, Bussy, Phil, Bensy, as well as some of my cousins, were all involved. I've seen them fight each other,

THE FIRST STEPS

for their gradings. They were tough men . . . are tough men. It was never wise getting on the wrong side of any of them.

I was caught shoplifting when I was seven years old. I saw my mates from school do it and thought they were pretty cool. My mum had given me $5 that day, so I went to the local shop. I knew the people who owned the shop, Kay and Larry — I saw them every day — and I tried to sneak this one lolly, a K-Bar, into my pocket. I didn't know what to do after that. I must have looked so dumb. I looked around, pretended that I wanted something, and walked out without buying anything. Larry came out and said to me, 'Show me what's in your pocket.' I said, 'Nothin'.' He used to think I was the nicest kid, and he said, 'Look, you're not like this.' He said he wouldn't call the police as long as I went home and told my mother what I had done. I told him I would.

I went home, going over and over in my head how I was going to tell her. In the end I didn't tell her. And, of course, she went to the shop the very next day.

I came home from school that afternoon. She was sitting, waiting for me, along with two of my uncles. Back in those days, a hiding was normal, and I got plenty from my mum. She was talented at sports and, as such, strong of hand. She was tough. It's been said to me my hips are rotated forward and my back's arched. I reckon that's because I was slapped so many times in the back by her when I was young, before I got too fast for her.

On this particular occasion, she left it to Uncle Phil.

'You get caught stealing yesterday?' she asked me. 'Yeah, I was going to tell you,' I replied. 'Alright,' she said. 'I'm going to get Uncle Phil to come over.'

Now, Phil was probably the roughest of the uncles with all the kids. Back in those days, if I started crying before I copped a hiding, sometimes my mum would be a little softer on me. She would say, 'I'm going to slap your behind.' I would burst into tears and she would go a little easier. This time, Uncle Phil said, 'Crying's not going to help you.'

It didn't. He said, 'You think stealing's cool, eh?' I tried to be brave, so I said, 'Yeah.' He said, 'Alright, I'm going to kick your bum so hard you can't sit down for two weeks.' He wasn't far off. I was never going to steal again. Ever.

It was the way we were hardened up. It was the way we learnt. And a lot of what I learnt back then made me the person I am today; with the values and the discipline I have. They came from the hidings I received, a lot of them.

All of my uncles had differing tempers. John was one of the most respected of my uncles. He was the New Zealand kickboxing champion for a long time. But he was probably the calmest out of all of them.

He has always given me advice, and never asks for anything from me. But all of my uncles taught me something. They all knew I didn't have a father around. Much of my competitiveness came from them. I wouldn't be who I am without them.

MY FIRST school was Apanui Primary, just around the corner from our house, which was at 10 Kiwi Street. While I loved my sport, I was also a good student. I always did my homework, and I particularly enjoyed maths.

I went to Whakatane Intermediate for two years, about a half-hour walk away. That was where I became more focused on rugby union, realising I was quite good at it. Then I moved on to Whakatane High School. A lot of my mates were solely focused on sport, but I enjoyed the schoolwork. I was a solid student with good grades. I represented my school in a maths competition called 24, held in a McDonald's restaurant in Rotorua. The idea is that you are given four numbers on a card and, using all of them, you have to find as many ways as possible to make 24, by adding, subtracting, multiplying or dividing. When you get to the higher levels you are given fractions. I finished second. I enjoyed maths, and I was good at it. No one could believe that then. A few probably wouldn't believe it now. I wanted to be an accountant for some time.

I also performed in our kapa haka, the Maori cultural dance group, competing against other schools in the Bay of Plenty and Waikato areas, practising for hours on end after school. The year it was in Whakatane, it was held at Rugby Park, and we performed in front of thousands of people.

I was also in the school choir. A few mates and I used to muck around with a guitar at school; the singing teacher heard us and asked us to join. We were reluctant at first, but when we were told that, every Thursday, from lunchtime to the end of school, we didn't have to go to class, we were sold. We learnt how to sing in harmony. I sang the melody in our barbershop group. We performed in a tournament in Hamilton, with combed hair and a kazoo.

But I became aware that sport was where I wanted to excel. I played most sports. I started playing rugby union when I was five years old, eventually developing into a fullback or a first five-eighth (fly-half). I would later represent Bay of Plenty, and was selected for a New Zealand under-15s team. I was meant to tour Australia, but the trip was cancelled. I ended up playing against another New Zealand invitational side at the Rugby Institute at Palmerston North. I played only one year of rugby league, when I was about seven, before my move to Australia. I don't remember much about playing league, but I know I was given the 'best tackler' award, which might amuse some.

I played basketball, volleyball, squash, tennis, touch football, of course, and golf. I competed in hoe waka (paddle canoe). The latter was a major part of Maori culture, and Whakatane High was one of the best exponents in New Zealand. I was just a skinny little kid, but I went fairly hard. A lot of the rugby union players used to paddle. Strength and timing were the keys. We practised every Thursday afternoon in the local river. Our crew competed in Hamilton and Auckland. We won Bay of Plenty and Waikato regional titles, but my broken collarbone meant I couldn't compete in the national competition.

Away from school I surfed, or at least tried to. Shane, the father of my little brothers Jeremy and Jordan, surfed every week. The three of us would join him, mostly at Ohope Beach, until I started putting more hours into rugby union. (I took surfing up again when I moved to the Gold Coast, until I was knocked out by my schoolmate's board and rescued by my friends.)

Through my school years in Whakatane I won a national volleyball title, two national touch football competitions and was runner-up in another.

I tried to play every sport I could. I thought it was important. And I used to watch every sport. If New Zealand were playing netball, I would watch it. If they were playing hockey . . .

I DIDN'T really have a choice about playing sport. My family has it in our blood. My uncles Luke and David were talented basketballers, Phil and Bensy were both strong rugby union talents, Bussy was the man at touch football and still plays a mean game of squash. Every time I go home, I keep my fitness up by playing squash with him. My mum played netball and touch

THE FIRST STEPS

football, as did all my aunties. One of my cousins, Maia Amai, has represented New Zealand in wheelchair basketball. She was burnt in a car when she was young and has not walked since. She's an inspiration to me. Another cousin, Tu Umaga-Marshall, plays rugby for the Canterbury Crusaders, having earlier played in the national basketball competition. I don't think there's a sport someone in our family has not played.

Sport was all I had apart from school. It was all I wanted to come home to. And we were always competitive. No one in my family enjoys losing. A few of my uncles found themselves in tussles with the referees in touch comps. That's how I learnt not to fight with referees, because you can be banned for a very long time, like Uncle Phil was.

Ever since I can remember, really, I was playing touch football with my family and at school. My family always tried to encourage the younger kids to play with the older kids or the adults.

I played most of my football on the oval just over the neighbour's back fence. The Whakatane touch football module was played there; Monday nights was mixed and Thursday nights both men's and women's. There were about six touch football fields there, and I was there most days of the week, playing with family or friends. My touch football background has been incredibly important in shaping what I do today. Look at the way I play: living on the edge a bit, taking risks. The flair, the flick passes — that sort of thing comes naturally. When you play touch football, it's harder to evade people, because all they have to do is touch you. It might hurt more, but it's easier to evade people in rugby league when they have to tackle you to stop you. Everything I would eventually do when I played rugby league came because of what I had learnt on the touch football oval. Touch has done wonders for me. But I have been playing it since I was five years old. I still practise it and it has just become second nature to me.

Having said that, I wasn't immediately successful. I didn't make any rep teams until I was about 13. By then I was trained by Moko Savage, a coach from Whakatane who used to work with the young kids in the area and put them in his teams, teaching them all the basics. He was the 'Godfather' of touch football back then. He trained a lot of young, raw talents and turned them into representative players. Moko was the coach of the Bay of Plenty under-18s side, which I represented when I was 13. I won a couple of New Zealand championships with that side. By the time I was 15, I was coach and manager of my school's mixed touch team. I'd decide on a training routine and the game plan when I was younger than some of my teammates. They still listened to me.

I'd been playing touch for my whole life, so I thought I knew everything. When we had to go away on trips, twice to Hamilton and also to Palmerston North, Uncle Phil would join us because we needed an adult around. By 15, I had also made the New Zealand under-19s squad, which played in the World Cup in 2001. We beat England 31–1, a record score.

That World Cup was the first time I ever pulled on the black jumper of New Zealand. I felt amazing, but I looked terrible. A skinny little kid, lucky to be 60 kg, with dyed-blond hair and regrowth coming through at the roots. I went through so many phases when I was younger: green hair, red hair, blue hair. My cousin Linda used to hook me up with all the styles. I had some of the worst cuts you have ever seen. My grandfather used to put a pot on my head and just shave around it. My Uncle Bussy used to make us shave our heads sometimes. I thought it was pretty cool at the time, but I look back on it now with embarrassment. For

A bouncing blond on the trampoline at Mick and Annalie's place.

With Mum and Dad at home.

With my mum, Lydia.

My third birthday, and one of Annalie's cakes. She's baked one, and I've eaten one, on all but a couple of my birthdays.

Above: On the tractor at the farm. I used to love helping Dad out.

Right: With Dad to my right and Michael, Uncle Bensy's son, to my left.

Keebra Park State High / Benji Marshall

The artwork I painted at Keebra Park as I was deciding whether to play for New Zealand or Australia. The colours — black, white, green and gold — symbolised the dilemma. The tribal symbols represent my family. 'Taonga' means sacred and special or treasured.

A rare sight, wearing the Australian coat of arms, with Drummayne 'Drummy' Dayberg during the touch football World Cup, in Japan in 2003.

The jersey from my Wests Tigers debut, framed and hung at Mum and Dad's house in Whakatane.

Mum and Dad at Christmas time.

With my mum and Koro Toby, who is flanked by my brothers Jeremy (green shirt) and Jordan (black shirt). My grandfather is rarely seen without his Wests Tigers shirt on these days.

Doherty Collection

With my cousins and brothers outside my Uncle Phil's house in Whakatane. Jeremy (green shirt) and Jordan (blue shirt) are in front of me. I'm holding my niece, Kalarney.

With my Uncle Bensy, his wife Michelle and their son Michael.

With my manager, Martin Tauber.

Action Photographics

School's out, and my debut's in; my first NRL match for the Tigers, on 27 July 2003. Terry Hill (with his arm around me in the bottom picture) used to drive me to training and was a constant source of amusement. He also backed me up in my first NRL fight.

Action Photographics

my first photo in a black jumper, there I am, with fake blond hair.

I had been to a camp with 19 others, and they were only picking 14 for the squad. It was one of my most nerve-wracking moments, waiting for the coach to phone me and tell me whether I was in the team or not. If the phone rang, I'd quickly pick it up. 'Hello. . . . Dammit.' Then I'd tell my aunty, who I was staying with, to quickly get off the phone because I was waiting for an important call. I finally got it, and I was nervous. The coach, John Whittaker, pulled the old, 'Look, it was a hard decision, I'm sorry to have to tell you that . . . you're in the team.' My heart sank as he was saying it. I was ready to cry. Then when he told me I'd made it, I was ecstatic. I told the whole family, and most of them came over for a barbecue to celebrate. I also had a couple of cousins who made the girls' under-18s team. Everyone was just so proud.

Receiving the tracksuit and the polo shirts was good enough. I was the youngest in the squad, and the smallest, and I didn't get measured up properly; my tracksuit was about three sizes too big for me.

No matter. My first game, in Auckland, was against Australia. Most of my family came to watch. We did the haka — the first time I had done it in New Zealand colours. It was very special, and I wanted more of it.

Lydia Marshall

I FIRST remember thinking Benj had some talent for sport when he was about four years old. Mick gave him a rugby ball. They would kick it, and throw it around at the farm. Then he started playing touch football for our family team when he was five or six. I was playing then. When he got to about nine or 10, he got a runaway try. I was the closest player in support, and I couldn't keep up with him. 'Hurry up, Mum,' he was yelling. My brothers were laughing at me as he did. I stopped playing after that. He might say he was slow at that age, but it was slow for him only. He was still quick.

I was 16 when I had Benj. When I found out I was pregnant, I thought to myself: 'I've got to tell somebody here.' I thought people were going to tell me to get rid of it. I told Mum. She just looked at me and shook her head. Then I ran into my dad. 'Oh, well, what are you going to do about it?' he asked. I was working at that stage, as a pool attendant. I'd finished school a few years earlier. 'What do you want to do?' he went on. I just said: 'I'm just going to keep it.'

My feeling was: I made my bed, I needed to lie in it. I just needed to carry on with life. You can't blame the kid that's in there. I thought: 'It's going to be a long road but this is what I want to do.' I never once thought about terminating it. I just couldn't do that.

The fact that Benj didn't know his father never bothered him. It still doesn't. His father knew I was pregnant, and did a runner. Someone said to me when Benj started playing league: 'You watch. He'll come back.' I said: 'Good luck. He'll get knocked out.' If my brothers don't do it, I'll do it myself. He has never come looking, though. He knows better, I think. That was his mistake. He gave up the best thing that could have happened to him.

I don't recall Benj ever asking me who his father was. As he got older, I think the thought just disappeared from his mind. It will never faze him. He had, and has, all his uncles. And he had the best man possible as a father in Mick.

Mick and Annalie did all the hard yards with me. They made it a lot easier for me when I was younger. I just look back now and think about how grateful I am. I know Benj feels the same. Mick had the biggest heart. He would give you his last dollar and the shirt off his back, too. He would have done anything for Benj.

THE FIRST STEPS

We would all go and watch him play rugby union. He would yell out: 'Mum!' Annalie and I would both turn to him. Everyone would be wondering what was going on. I never minded at all that he called Annalie 'Mum'. She was one of the best things to happen to Benj and me.

I'm also very lucky I had my mum and dad. Benj was very spoilt by my mother. He wouldn't remember. She would carry him everywhere. My dad was the same; he was the first to hold him when I walked out of the hospital.

My mum got breast cancer when Benj was still quite young, and Annalie and Mick were a tower of strength for me. He'd go to their place for the weekend, or even a week if need be. I was looking after my mother as well. My sisters would give me a hand, to give me a bit of a break. I had to bath Mum, and when she started to get worse, she was in so much pain. Benj was not even 18 months; I was trying to feed him and look after Mum.

When Mum got very sick, I had to ask Annalie to look after Benj for a bit longer. My sisters who had children had their hands full with theirs and my sister who didn't have any was living in Australia.

Once he could walk and talk, Benj was independent. He knew what he wanted and where he wanted to go. He'd go to Annalie's or Bensy's or his Uncle Phil's. They'd ring up and say: 'Benj is here.' I couldn't lock him up because he would have found a way to get out.

He was a good kid growing up. He had some mates who used to get in a bit of trouble. But he was smart enough to know what he wanted. He'd know he'd have his uncles to answer to if he joined in. After a while, I'd never even have to threaten him with them. It just grew out of him. I only had to worry about him dyeing his hair pink or green. As long as he had his sport . . . he was playing so many too: cricket, basketball, rugby union, touch football.

He works hard. He pushes himself as hard as he can, because there's a level that he wants to be at. He'll strive to be where he thinks he should be, not where others do. He's been like that since he was young.

The only occasions he worries about what others think of him are when people try to tell him that he can't do something. He wants to prove to everyone that he can do it. That's something he's always done; the more you say he can't do it, the more he will prove you wrong. That's why I'd tell him he can't do the dishes. Once, when he was playing rugby union — he would have been nine years old — he was told he couldn't play halfback. But he wanted to. So over the next couple of weeks, he proved them wrong. From then on, he played halfback.

That attitude has helped him through his injuries. There have been times I'd ring him, and I knew he was in his room, lying on the bed, staring at the ceiling. I could tell by the echo. The first shoulder injury wasn't too bad, but then the second one, and the third one, and the fourth one . . . 'Where's this going?' But I knew he'd get through it.

Chapter 2

A Golden Age

THE FIRST batch of training gear I sent to my family was actually the lime green of Canberra. I arrived on the Gold Coast, having taken up a scholarship with Keebra Park State High, and the school was linked with the Raiders. Back then, in 2002, my relatives were hoping I'd do well enough to play for the Raiders. Then about three months after I started at the school, Canberra pulled out of the school programme, and I thought I'd have to return home, as I thought the scholarship was finished. But Wests Tigers, who were coached by Terry Lamb at the time, linked with the school. I remember watching the television news report, not long after Terry was sacked. Tim Sheens had been appointed. I took an interest because I knew it could be the club I would join. I used to watch all their games, and study the players.

The first time I met Tim, I recall, was at a schoolboys' carnival, which he came to watch on the Gold Coast. He visited the school to talk to us. I shook his hand, but I was too shy to say anything to him. He told me that the club had a 'cubs' team and he wanted me to play for it. I came down to Sydney for a few weeks in the off-season, and I represented Wests Tigers for the first time in the 2003 Sevens tournament.

That was an eye-opener. I was suddenly matched up against men. I'd been used to that, but this was different. They were bigger, faster and stronger than anyone I'd been up against before. I was light, too, about 74 kg. It was scary; I simply wasn't used to the kind of battering that these guys could dish out.

The first NRL player I tackled was Steve Simpson, of the Newcastle Knights. Let me tell you, it was the nastiest feeling that I've ever experienced. I just stood in front of him in the hope of getting him down; I was holding on for grim life, and he dragged me about 10 metres while I waited for one of my teammates to finally come and finish the job. 'How am I going to get through this?' I thought to myself. I weighed about 30 kg less than Steve Simpson, and I had to match it with him, a concrete block of footballer.

Playing against such big-name players felt very weird. Tim threw a lot of young players into that tournament, but we went okay. Midway through that year, I travelled to Sydney for the cubs camp. I trained for two days with the rest of the younger guys and then we played in a match against the Roosters at Campbelltown, before the first-grade game. That cubs team included guys who have been my teammates for many years, Liam Fulton, Bryce Gibbs and Robbie Farah. I scored four tries, and I was taken off with 20 minutes to go. A few of the first-graders were watching the game, and Ben Galea, Darren Senter and Mark O'Neill congratulated me. They were guys I'd only seen before on television, watching back at home on the Gold Coast.

I MUST have been destined to play rugby league. How did I come to be at Campbelltown that day, meeting all those people

I had looked up to? If it wasn't for something as obscure as a high school tourism excursion, I mightn't have even played rugby league, let alone done so for the Tigers.

Before all of that, back in New Zealand, I studied tourism at Whakatane High School, and at the end of every year, the students who did the subject would go on an excursion. In late 2001, about 30 of us visited the Gold Coast to have a look at the likes of Movie World and Dreamworld (truth be told, I chose the subject because of the trip). But a rugby league trial match was thrown into the schedule very late and unofficially. One of my mates, who used to go to Whakatane High, had moved to the Gold Coast and was at Keebra Park High School, which was in Southport. The Keebra coaching staff asked our teachers if any of us played at all, the match being a trial. They found three of us some boots and we had a game against one of the Canberra Raiders junior rep sides.

I was actually quite lost playing league; I didn't know what to do. In New Zealand, I generally only watched rugby league if the Warriors were winning. I used to watch all the Kiwis' games. It did intrigue me; it was similar to touch football, with six tackles. But it just wasn't as popular when I lived in Whakatane, and I'd hardly played the sport.

The Keebra Park coach, Greg Lenton, threw me in at halfback. He said to me, 'Alright, you're a bit lost, but just pick up the ball and have a run.' So I picked up the ball from a scrum, stepped maybe five players and scored a try. After that, he pulled me aside and said, 'Where's that been?' I replied, 'I didn't know that's what you wanted.' Greg asked three of us to come back on scholarship at the school. I had two weeks to decide. I thought I could give it a go and if it didn't work out, I could return home and play rugby union.

I had started hanging out with a bad crowd in New Zealand. I was too scared of what Uncle Phil would do to me to join in anything too serious, but I saw a lot of bad stuff happen: burgling houses, smoking marijuana and smashing shop windows. A lot of them used to meet down at the park for fights among the town gangs. My mates used to send me home before the fighting started. Most of them knew who my uncles were and they wouldn't dare try anything on me. On my way home, I'd turn around to see the fighting start. You could describe it as organised chaos. Or just a royal rumble. That's how it was. Not now, but then.

There wasn't a lot of opportunity in Whakatane, and going to Keebra Park meant my schooling would be paid for. I felt like I had nothing to lose. Except my family, of course. Leaving was one of the hardest things that I have done. My mum was at home with my two little brothers, Jordan and Jeremy. She was a single mum, and I was going to miss out on my brothers growing up. I was very hesitant. My mum was crying, and when Jordan, who would have been about nine, said to me, 'Don't worry, I'll be the man of the house now,' I just lost it. I was scared. I cried in my mum's arms, but she packed my bags and made sure I boarded the plane. I had no choice.

MY BROTHERS and I were close. I had been looking after them on my own sometimes from the time I was 11 or 12. I fed them, took them to the toilet, wiped their bottoms; did all the things I would have done if I was their father.

I took them to the swimming pool and watched them. It's what it was. I took them under my wing and babysat them.

Jordan is eight years younger than I am, and Jeremy's 11 years my junior. They were still tiny when I left. Because I was so used to being there for them, and being like a father, it was extremely hard to leave, knowing Jordan was going to have to do what I did for Jeremy: to stand up and be a man.

And I was on my own at the same time. Actually, that's not entirely true. The two other boys who played in the trial, Tamati Coates, who was my best mate from high school in Whakatane, and Taj Bullivant, came with me, and I did know some people who played touch football on the Gold Coast. I was billeted with a family in Nerang for the first year and a half. Their eldest two sons went to Keebra Park and their youngest son and daughter would later go there.

It was hard, arriving on some stranger's doorstep. But at the same time, I had been forever moving around, so it was nothing new to me.

I worked at Hungry Jack's, doing the midnight to 7 a.m. shift on weekends, to pay the family, until I was sacked for giving my friends a little extra (a triple Whopper, I recall, with all the trimmings) on occasion after they had nights out in Surfers Paradise. My first introduction to real work came via a New Zealander I'd met playing rugby union in Coolangatta. His name was Paris Kingi, and he owned a concreting business. I knew his father.

A fledgling concreter's first job is almost always just taking the wheelbarrow and dumping the load of concrete. They filled it right to the top, and conveniently forgot to tell me the golden rule, that if your wheelbarrow's going to fall over, you just have to let it go. I was probably 74 kg then, carrying this wheelbarrow full of cement, struggling as I tried to hold onto it. And sure enough it toppled over, taking me over with it. I ended up in the freshly laid concrete. The next week, one of the concreters, Mick, went into K-Mart and bought a Bob the Builder toy wheelbarrow. When I arrived for work I said, 'What am I doing today?' I went over to the truck and waiting for me was a plastic wheelbarrow.

I ended up moving in with Paris for a while. He bought me a little four-speed Mitsubishi Mirage so I could drive the half-hour from Coolangatta to Keebra Park and back at night. I could work with him on Tuesdays, when the school allowed the kids who were playing league to do so, and weekends. I made some money, although I never had a lot of it.

THERE WERE stages when I did it tough. I wanted to go home on so many occasions, but I just wanted to prove people wrong. Even my uncles said, 'You'll be back in a year.' As soon as someone says I can't do something, it makes me want to do it more, especially if it's my uncles saying it. 'Who wants to go to the shop? I'll time you, see how fast you can go,' they would tell me. I'd go.

At one stage, Mum and Dad (Mick and Annalie) came over, and they wanted to take me home. They saw where I was living and what was going on, when I was living with one of my mates early on. They didn't like that I didn't have much money. But there was no way I was going to go home.

It was made easier by the people I knew. One of my close friends, Kane George, used to take me out and pay for me. A lot of people had my back. I was blessed that I had so many people who were willing to help me onto the path that I'm on now. I haven't forgotten any of them. If it wasn't for their help, I could have been eating off the street on some occasions. There are so many people that I owe a lot to.

Particularly Paris. He had a large extended family, and many of them lived in the same part of Coolangatta, kind of like a village of east coast New Zealanders. Many of them were concreters.

Tamati and I would eat and stay, more often than not, either with Paris or another family, Jehovah's Witnesses and talented musicians who we called Uncle Chiefy and Aunty Janet. Their children all played in bands: Isaac played guitar and drums, Leon guitar, their youngest Paerau drums and bass. Leon taught me how to play riffs on guitar. Runs of blues notes. He let me play bass at a couple of gigs, just birthdays and the like. Leon taught me a lot when it came to music, and Isaac is a great singer. He'd write his own songs and record them on his mixer. Leon let me record a song, about girls. They always were about girls. We lost the lyrics, so there's no evidence of it as far as I'm aware.

I always loved playing the guitar, as well as the keyboard. I'm not a particularly good singer, but I enjoy it. I can't read music, but Leon, who lived in a granny flat with his wife Suzy, taught me the chords and scales.

I used music as a way of getting away from everything else. For us, weekends were rugby during the day on Saturday, then home for a jamming session. They had set up drums, guitars and a microphone. There would be a keg as well so we could have a few beers while we played or sang. The families would come together on Sunday as well for a barbecue and a few beers.

I must admit, they weren't the only beers I enjoyed. Paris and the other guys in the rugby team used to take me out to the pubs. I was 16 and used a fake ID. The security guard at the Coolangatta Sands Hotel, Matty, thought I was 20 when I first met him. On my eighteenth birthday, about two years later, I handed him my real ID. 'You've been coming here for two years,' he told me, stunned.

Coolangatta was where I spent my first, and only, night in a cell. I fell asleep in the bushes during a night out and the police threw me in the lock-up for the night to have a sleep. When I woke up, they let me go.

SOME OF my first, and I'd like to think finest, performances at the school were not carried out on grass but on wooden floors or concrete.

Two of my mates, Nigel Fruean and Harley Williams, and I used to play guitar and sing regularly. We sang at the Keebra Park awards night, with Jenna Feros, who always used to sing by herself, never in front of others. We sang 'One Sweet Day', by Mariah Carey with Boyz II Men. We rehearsed every day in the lead-up to it, most of which didn't go too smoothly. Not long before the awards night, Annalie's mum had passed away, so I dedicated the song to her, as well as other family members. Nigel and Harley could really sing. I still had a high-pitched voice and I tried hard. We received a standing ovation.

I liked to make what ordinarily might be considered alternative things to do. No one messed with the football players so if we sang, it was cool. We sang in the playground. We sang in the Gold Coast hinterland, on a biology field trip to study bilbies. Around the campfire, Harley and I made up a song about the little marsupial. The school bribed us with a $20 tuckshop voucher to make us sing in front of a conference of school principals at Jupiter's Casino.

I didn't care what anyone else thought. At the time we didn't realise the impact we were having, but by the end the principal, Fran Jones, was thanking us for changing perceptions. Why not sing? Why not dance?

I also liked dancing. Back in New Zealand, my mate Wiremu Bennett and I used to breakdance. There wasn't much to do in Whakatane, so when a group of breakdancers visited the school and put on a show, 'Woody' and I wanted in. The group ran some clinics to try to get the kids into hip-hop dancing and breakdancing. Every morning, we'd go to school early to practise, and then do the same after the final bell. We used to put cardboard boxes on the concrete so we didn't scrape ourselves. Or we'd go to the gymnasium if it was free, practising on the wooden floors. It was already cool when I started doing it.

In Australia it was a little different. If you were part of the football culture, you were frowned upon if you danced. At a blue-light disco, all the footy boys stood in the corner, so my Kiwi mates and I put on a bit of a breakdancing show. By the end of the song, most of the kids in the room had circled around us.

I'm not sure why the other kids looked down upon us for doing it. They used to say dancing was 'gay', but I found, funnily enough, that it was a good way to get the girls. I chose dancing as a subject. I loved it. It was another way of doing something sporty during school hours. To me, it was normal, because I had been doing it for years, but to others, it was weird.

The funny thing was, though, because my Kiwi mates and I were in the football team, other kids looked up to us. Half the boys in the team chose dancing as a subject as well. I guess I wanted to change perceptions. By doing the subject we made dancing look cool to others. It was a great way to get away from schoolwork for a period. Half of them ended up in a high school performing arts competition, a Rock Eisteddfod. With me.

I went in 2003. I was close with one of the teachers who was heavily involved in the rock eisteddfod group. Miss Anne Pike asked a group of us to do an audition. So we made up our own R&B and breakdance routine, danced in the gym in front of the teachers, and made it into the group.

We had to dress up as cowboys, with vest (no shirt), cowboy pants, cowboy hat . . . and we were dancing to the song 'Cotton Eye Joe'. 'Where did you come from, where did you go? Where did you come from, Cotton Eye Joe?' Just imagine it. My friends and I were told, effectively, to do our own thing, right at the start of the routine. I wanted to come on, front and centre, and do some moves, with my mates joining me. We all rehearsed for an hour most afternoons, and for three hours one day a week, for about eight weeks, before we travelled to Brisbane to perform at the Entertainment Centre.

It was an experience and a half. I made up a rule on the bus that every boy had to sit next to a girl. All the boys tried to sneak a peek of the girls behind the thin curtains that separated the makeshift changing rooms. My mates and I had a guitar, so we positioned ourselves in a thoroughfare while we sang Craig David songs. We had 50 or 60 people standing around watching us by the end.

Our rehearsal was poor. The girls were crying. And then our performance proper came around. It was a different kind of nervousness than I'd ever experienced. I'd played at Suncorp Stadium in front of a fairly sizeable crowd by that stage. But on this occasion, I was out of my comfort zone. The Brisbane Entertainment Centre was full, and I was first on stage in our performance. As I was doing a breakdancing move called a 'windmill', the crowd cheered wildly. We didn't win, but it was a great experience. The footy players still participate in rock eisteddfods. I look back with pride that they do so partly because of me.

OF COURSE, league was still king. It wasn't hard to pick the members of the team, because we all used to have to wear our footy shorts as part of the school uniform.

I was lucky; I literally had the keys to the school. I knew the alarm code to the school, and the music teacher would often leave me the key to the music room to use in the lunch break or after school. I had the keys to the showers as well. Greg Lenton, the league coach, and another teacher, Peter Craig, made sure all the little things were in place for us to thrive.

Peter almost cancelled my scholarship not long after I arrived. I played up a few times at the start. I'd only just started playing rugby league and I didn't understand the game or the culture. I do not believe you can understand the league culture unless you are a part of it. Mr Craig and I butted heads all the time in the beginning. By the time I'd been there for six months, it wasn't hard to realise what I needed to do. I knew that strong leadership was important.

Greg was a huge influence, of course. He always had my back. If someone bagged me, he'd set them straight. When I first arrived, people would tell me, 'Don't get on his bad side, he's a grumpy man.' I never saw that side of him. I think he had a soft spot for me; he was always so honest with me. And he always had faith in me. A lot of people were telling him he shouldn't have been playing me, or that I was out of position.

But he stuck to his convictions — 'I'm playing him at five-eighth.' He copped a lot of criticism when it came to me, about the way I played. I'd see it on his face. He'd say, 'You wouldn't believe the stuff I heard on the weekend.' The way I played was never what you'd call conventional rugby league — and at that time, conventional was in: five up for a kick, no shifts. I had to get used to the game, but all I wanted to do was shift the ball, step some defenders, and chip and chase on the second tackle.

And Greg used to back me. He was the one who taught me to play what I see. Some coaches try to strangle it and some try to harness it. He made me confident in my own ability. I was always a confident player, but he showed confidence in me. If anyone had tried to coach that out of me, I probably would have left the school, and I could have been writing a completely different story. He just let me run with it, literally. He had faith in me, and I was able to learn by experience. When I see him, even now, he'll say, 'What's your strength?' I'll say, 'My running game.' He was my first real league coach.

But he was more than a coach. He'd offer me money if he thought I needed it. If I had no lunch, he would let me use his tab at the tuckshop. And he made sure I practised for at least three hours a day when I was at school, because I was new to rugby league. But he also checked my class attendance records.

Rugby league was Greg's baby. It was a subject at Keebra Park, part of the timetable. I could start school with PE, then have rugby league, maths, English and science, which meant I could be outside for two periods a day. It was a great place to go to school, a great place to learn rugby league. But if you didn't do your schoolwork, or you missed classes, you didn't play. That's what I liked about it. I have a lot of pride, too, knowing that the rugby league programme at the school is flying, and that I had a part to play. I was there for two years; I actually repeated Year 12 so I could play again. I didn't mind doing it, because I spent a lot of the first year getting used to the Australian way of teaching. I consider myself lucky to have done it. I loved it at school, and I will never forget the years at Keebra. I was treated well. And of course, the other kids worshipped the guys in the footy team, which included the likes of Rangi Chase, Sam Moa and Greg Eastwood. Greg was 15 and playing in the top team.

Some of the teachers didn't like us much, but they were in the minority. I never really acted like a footy student. I used to hang out with a lot of the teachers. Miss Pike, who ran the art department, knew I didn't have any parents looking after me, or any family for that matter, so she used to make me cakes, and bring me lunch. I used her account at the canteen. 'Put that on Miss Pike's tab, please.' At lunchtime sometimes, instead of hanging out in the playground, I would stay in the staff room. She had a fridge in her office which was filled with other teachers' food, and which I used to eat. If I was feeling stressed or pressured, I'd go to her office.

I used to get homesick all the time. None of my family was near me. I telephoned home from the school once a week. Miss Pike used to look after me. She was like a mum for me at school. The principal, Fran, made life so much easier for me. The other kids used to think she was grumpy, but I didn't.

I had spent most of my childhood hanging out with older people, so I was used to acting like one. I knew I had to tough it out, and I wouldn't be here if I didn't.

Greg Lenton

BENJI MARSHALL was awful the first time I saw him play rugby league. But for five minutes he was brilliant. That was all I needed to see to know he had talent.

We were due to have a trial against a development squad from Canberra. We were linked with the Raiders prior to Wests Tigers, through another former student Jamahl Lolesi, who played at Canberra. Around the same time, a guy I knew from around Whakatane was due to bring a group of kids over for a tourism excursion. He telephoned me and asked if he could have a look at the school. I asked him if he had any footballers who'd like to have a run.

A few of them played in the trial, at the local Southport Tigers' ground. One of them was a skinny, fuzzy-haired boy who just did not have a clue. He was terrible. He didn't — couldn't — get near the football, and looked like he knew nothing at all about the game. Of course, I found out later he actually didn't, not having played the sport much previously. I had to take him off quite early.

With about 10 minutes remaining, I saw him sitting on the sideline, surrounded by about 40 other kids. I could see the little face looking at me, with big eyes. I remember someone saying to me, 'He's quick.' I decided to put him in at halfback for five minutes so he could at least get his hands on the ball. But I really didn't think too much of it. He picked up the ball from the scrum-base a few minutes later and stepped his way through the Canberra team to score, running about 50 metres. He was certainly quick and he did have feet on him. There was something there, I remember thinking. I asked him if he wanted to enrol at the school. He turned up a few weeks later, straight from the airport, with a leather bag with a couple of photos of his brothers and a few bits of clothing in it. That's where it all started.

It was a battle. Not many people rated Benji. When we were in between Canberra and Wests Tigers, we were up at Logan for a game, and I said to one of the Brisbane Broncos' staff, 'What do you think of him?' 'No,' he said to me. 'But I like that kid over there.' He was pointing at Greg Eastwood. A few years later, I was in the boardroom at the Broncos, and I was asked in no uncertain terms why Benji went to the Tigers and not the Broncos. A coach once sat in the Keebra Park staff room and told me Benji wouldn't make his local club side. From day one with him, there was enormous resistance. I tell the kids to this day: 'The problem is you all see Benji Marshall as a superstar. You all think it was easy for him. It was harder for him than most of you guys. When he was here he wasn't a superstar. It was worse for him because he played the game differently.'

'What's all that nonsense he's doing?' I'd be told. He copped so much flak, even from inside the school walls, from parents of kids who might have played the game more traditionally. He was a target. The number of phone calls I got from him at night, when he was down . . . I'm always interested to watch him now, such a confident young man. Yet the kid I knew was more brittle.

But he worked hard. I'd be walking up the hill away from the oval after training, and I'd turn around and he'd be kicking at the goalposts. It was a long, slow process with him. He was so raw. He was a touch player. In those days touch players were not highly rated. But I decided very early in the piece that I was better off trying to enhance what he had rather than trying to change him. So many people tried to tell me I had to change him: 'He's got to stop doing that.' 'He's got to stop doing this.' But I resisted. I thought he had something unique. I remembered a story I'd heard about John McEnroe, whose father was looking for a coach for him. McEnroe had an unconventional serve, and most of the coaches wanted to change it. Then one of the coaches said, 'I can work with that.' His father said: 'You've got the job.' The way I saw Benji, if a few things went his way, he could do anything.

He never cut corners. He was driven by making sure that his brothers never went through what he did. He would say that to me so many times. For a long time, he didn't want anyone to know about his background, what he came from. I don't think he wanted to know. I think he painted a picture in his mind about what happened, which was different to what really did happen.

And he was a trailblazer, in some respects. There weren't many Kiwi boys in the schools in those days, and he was the target of racial abuse, from the crowds. He had to deal with that as well as being different in the way that he played. Not only was he different, he was black.

He'd get upset from time to time, but he learnt to deal with it. There were always two personalities. There would be one for out there, and the real one. I don't think that's ever changed. I think he learnt from a very early age that he had to build a wall between the wider population and his real persona, to protect himself. He certainly learnt to put a few more bricks in it at Keebra Park, as the attention started coming his way.

I very quickly told Terry Lamb, the Tigers coach when we linked with the club, about Benji. He was in his first year with us, and was still very thin and raw. By the time Tim Sheens took over, he knew about him, too. At the end of 2002, Benji's first year at the school, Tim came up to the Gold Coast and wanted to take Benji back with him. I sat in the principal's office while I talked to Tim and Steve Lavers. Benji was in another office at the other end of the hallway. I told them: 'I know kids, and this kid's not ready.' I walked into the other office and Benji was as white as a sheet. He was excited, but when I told him he was staying for another year, I could see the relief on his face.

I always thought Benji's vision was his great gift, even though his step, his flick and his speed are all eye-catching. Most people would say he was off the cuff and instinctive, and that always used to get to me. Benj has what I would term a sporting literacy. He would come up with plays, and the people watching would tell me it was off the cuff. I'd say: 'No it wasn't. He saw that guy long before the guy was there.' When he was playing, balls would be constantly hitting the deck, because the players with him weren't capable of being where he knew they should have been, even though he played with some very good footballers.

The graphs and charts happen in his brain, and they happen at a thousand miles an hour. It's not off the cuff. He's got a computer and a half stored in his head. He was a bright student and he is a bright footballer. The step helped him at the start, because it got people watching him. I probably wouldn't have looked twice at him that day at Southport, if it wasn't for that step. You could say that his step made him famous. But his brain made him.

Chapter 3

Tiger Cub

I'M SUSPICIOUS of private phone numbers at the best of times. After the cubs trial against the Roosters, Tim Sheens told me he'd bring me back down to Sydney sometime in the off-season. But a few weeks later, after I'd gone back to school, a call came through on my mobile phone.

'Benji, it's Tim Sheens.' Now, it just so happened that not long before that, a couple of my mates had been joking about what I would do if Tim Sheens called me and asked me to play in the NRL. So, thinking it was my mates, I said, 'Yeah, whatever,' threw a couple of swear words at the voice on the other end of the line, before hanging up. The phone rang again, and the voice said: 'Trust me. You don't want to hang up this time.' 'Who's this?' I replied. After he said, 'Tim Sheens,' I said, 'Don't lie, who is it?' He said, 'It's Tim Sheens, and if you hang up, you're going to regret it.'

Now realising I had just sworn at an NRL coach, not to mention hung up in his face, I quickly apologised and allowed him to continue. 'I need you to keep this to yourself. Can you keep a secret?' he said. 'Yeah, man, I can keep a secret,' I answered. 'I'm going to play you next week, at halfback, against Newcastle.' I said, 'Huh, against Andrew Johns?' 'Yeah, against

Andrew Johns. But you can't tell anyone,' he said. 'Don't even tell your mother.'

I hung up and started jumping around the room. I rang my mum straight away, as well as my uncles. I pretty much told my entire family. A few of them didn't believe me. I had to ring my Uncle John and say, 'Tell them I'm not lying, I'm going to play.' They knew I wouldn't lie to him.

I went to school on Monday, Tuesday and Wednesday, flew down and trained with the team on Thursday and Saturday and played on Sunday. I looked forward to the private number coming up on the phone after that.

TIM ENDED up starting me off the bench, and told me I might get only 10 or 20 minutes. 'I can't promise anything,' he said. But 20 minutes into the first half, he told me to start warming up. 'I'm going to take Robert Miles off,' he said. 'So where am I playing?' I asked. 'Fullback.' So after training me at halfback, I made my first NRL appearance at fullback. 'You'll be right,' he told me.

I was petrified. We were defending, and almost immediately Newcastle made a break. There was one man to beat, me, and I missed the tackle, allowing them to score. I had been on the field about 20 seconds. What an introduction to first grade. After their next set, one of the boys said to me, 'Just have a run.' I stepped a few of them — I remember Matt Gidley was one of them — but then Ben Kennedy rag-dolled me and said, 'Welcome to first grade.'

I played about 50 minutes that day. For the last 10 minutes, I replaced Lincoln Withers at halfback and directed the team around. I have watched the video of that debut countless times.

Annalie used to tape all the games, and I'd go home at Christmas and watch them all, trying to figure out how to get better. I look back now and wonder why there was such a fuss.

I DIDN'T really know what to expect afterwards. The whole experience was new to me. The media was waiting for me outside the dressing room, and there were flashing cameras as I came out of the door in the Tigers team uniform, which back then was an awful purple shirt with black leather jacket.

When you walk out at Campbelltown, all the supporters wait outside the door. I'd soaked the whole experience up for a fair while inside, talking to Tim and meeting some of the other staff. I thought all the fans would be gone by the time I walked out. But waiting for me was a cheer like I'd never heard before, and a line of people from the dressing-room door to the gate, all wanting my autograph and photos. There were young girls throwing themselves at me, giving me kisses. People were calling out my name. It was surreal. I had been at school only a few days earlier. I loved it. 'How good's this?' I thought to myself. I'll never forget that feeling.

I was back at school the next day, a little bit hung over, I've got to admit. Steve Lavers was the Tigers' football manager at the time, and he told me there was a bit of interest in me. I got straight off the plane, headed to school, still with my kit bag, and a half a dozen or so TV cameras were waiting for me, along with photographers. They followed me wherever I went. I felt like a superstar walking through an airport being followed by the paparazzi. By this stage, the school bell had rung, but nobody had gone to class. Most of the students were still waiting on the netball courts, through the school gates, cheering, clapping and chanting, 'Keebra Park'. I did not know what to do. I almost started crying, which would have been a sight for the cameras. I was taken into the school offices and Greg Lenton congratulated me; he normally doesn't show much emotion, but he gave me a hug and told me how proud he was of me.

I remember him saying: 'Look, things are going to change around here. We might have to get you some security.' Then he said, 'You don't have to do any schoolwork today.' I spent much of the day doing interviews. The principal, Fran Jones, congratulated me and said, 'You've done the school so proud — you've put Keebra Park on the map.' She told me to mention the school and education whenever I could. The exposure all came fairly naturally to me. It was at that moment that I realised I quite enjoyed being in front of a camera.

I had print photographers making me sit in class with my schoolbooks pretending I was writing; they put me in a class with a whole heap of kids with glasses, I can only assume to make me look smart. Then they made me go outside and take my shirt off; a little skinny 76 kg runt with a terrible haircut and a tattoo on his arm, throwing the ball up in the air for the cameras.

The tattoo was a mistake. I had asked my mum at 15 if I could have one. My cousin was getting one, and I thought it'd be pretty cool for me to have one as well. Mum wasn't happy about it at first, but she relented. I offered the tattoo artist, from a town called Kawerau — about 20 minutes out of Whakatane — an old television, which had been broken, mind you, as payment for it. And that was it. My first tattoo, on my left arm.

I thought it was mad at the time, and I made up all these stories about what the design meant. It actually meant absolutely nothing — I just liked the look of the tribal design — but I told people one line was my mum, another was my brothers, and the circle was my family and where I'm from. I showed my cousins and they said: 'Yeah, that's so mean.' I showed my uncles and they said: 'That's ugly, bro.' They still tease me. It was one of the biggest mistakes I made. I regret it. It doesn't mean anything, but all the tattoos I have gotten since have meaning.

AFTER MY debut, I started getting noticed straight away, even just walking down the street. 'You're that guy.' I wondered, 'How do these people know who I am?' Girls at school even started writing me love letters; there would be girls coming down to the footy tunnel saying, 'My friend likes you.' From a fairly normal schoolkid, who nobody really took much notice of, to a life of attention, of cameras, all within a few hours. It was crazy.

Tim told me he wasn't going to use me the following weekend, to keep the media away from me, but he planned to use me the week after, against Brisbane at Suncorp Stadium. 'What, against Darren Lockyer?'

So the weekend after my debut, I played for the school at Suncorp, against Wavell High School, in a match to make the Queensland schoolboys final. We lost. So from walking through the tunnel at Suncorp Stadium, playing kids I hardly knew, to doing the same thing just a week later, playing halfback against someone I had idolised. There was Lockyer, of course, and Tonie Carroll. We were down in a tight game, with just a few minutes to go. On the last tackle, I was dummy half, and the Broncos all rushed out of the line; I made a line break, stepped Lockyer, only to be pulled down just before the line. Chris Heighington scored the winning try. I'd won two in a row. 'How good's this?' I thought.

I went back to school and the media hype seemed bigger than two weeks earlier. By this stage, I was like a little kid in a candy store. I was loving it. 'Photo shoot, yeah you want a photo? Yep, I'm coming.' 'You, yep, I'll be two minutes.' I was being pulled everywhere, but it was great. I was trying to soak up everything. Here I was, a kid earning about $6000 a year concreting, being treated like a star. So much so that when I went back to work a few days later, Mick, who had given me the Bob the Builder wheelbarrow, replaced it with a real one. 'There you go, you're a man now,' he said. He was a Broncos fan.

I played another two games that year, winning one against the Cowboys and losing another against Penrith. Tim rang me two days before we were due to play the Cowboys, telling me Lincoln Withers had been injured and I needed to play halfback. Train one day, play, then home the next day.

I'd stay at Steve Lavers' place at Narrabeen and Terry Hill, who lived on the Northern Beaches, would give me a lift to training. Terry took me under his wing — and helped me after my first NRL fight. When we played the Cowboys, there was a push and shove early on between David Myles, who was playing five-eighth, and me. I cocked my fists at him and he said, 'Go on, punch me.' I threw one, and he hit me straight on the nose, which started bleeding.

Terry ran in and started laying into my opponent. And then for the rest of the game, Terry sledged David Myles mercilessly. With his lisp, he'd say, 'He's a th-choolkid — you're getting shown up by a th-choolkid. Look at him, he's a th-choolkid. You're getting th-moked by a th-choolkid'. He was always there for me though, as were guys like Mark O'Neill, Ben Galea and Corey Pearson. They certainly helped me through my introduction to first grade.

The other guys weren't really used to having me there, but I was just so confident I didn't let that get to me. All I knew back then was how to run the ball. I wasn't much of a ballplayer. I was sticking to what I knew, and that was to run the ball. And it was working. I later signed a new contract with the Tigers, on a lot more money than I had been used to, about $50,000 with some incentives. I felt like I was signing into a different life. I played in the World Sevens in early 2004; we'd just signed Pat Richards, Scott Sattler and Scott Prince. We won that tournament, and they haven't held another one since, so I still regard us as the reigning world rugby league sevens champions.

That was the start of it all. There are still things I am not used to. It was a rapid rise, from concreting, or trying to concrete, to playing in an NRL team in what felt like no time at all. One day, I'm at a mate's place in Campsie ordering Chinese for lunch — no one knowing me, and no one looking at me — and the next I was playing first grade. I would turn the TV on and I felt like I couldn't get away from myself. It was weird. I still watched it, because I liked it. It was amazing. From one day to the next, everything changed.

A management decision

AFTER I made my first-grade debut, I had a lot of people telling me that they wanted to be my manager. They promised me this, they promised me that. At the time, the Internet was taking off, so I Googled what managers are meant to do and how much commission they take. I read stories about NFL players who were ripped off by their managers, and stories about footballers who retired with little or no money. If I'm not sure of something, I will always attempt to find out about it. I just didn't know a great deal about what managers are meant to do, but I knew that

I would need one. I had emails from prospective managers, and mates phoning me saying they had friends who wanted to look after me. Some managers were offering some of my friends cash if they were able to convince me to sign with them.

I didn't know who any of them were; I didn't know what they were about. I decided I wanted to meet them first. I sat down with Greg Lenton and Peter Craig, who had negotiated my initial deal with the Tigers, giving me enough money to live off. They asked me what I wanted to achieve out of my career. I told them I wanted to be able to buy my family a house, and live well myself. When I retired, I didn't want to be in a position where I had nothing to show for my career. I decided that I'd give a number of managers something of a questionnaire. Call it a tender process. I gave them a list of scenarios, things like: 'If I made $100,000, what would you let me do with the money?'

Some of the managers didn't respond. I arranged to meet the ones who did. Some said because I was only young, I should have a bit of fun with my money at first in Sydney. That wasn't what I wanted. I am bad with money. If I have it available to me, I will spend it. I'm too generous with it. I'd spend it myself or give it to others. I spend more money on others than I do on myself. But I don't mind at all. I'm willing to help anyone out because so many helped me when I had nothing. I know that if I was in their shoes and they were in mine, they would put their hand in their pocket. That's what mates do. It's how I was raised.

And so I met Martin Tauber, who had responded with a 20-or-so-page document in response to the different scenarios I had put to him. He broke it down dollar by dollar; put x-amount of the money here to save for a deposit for a house, y-amount into the sharemarket. I would get an allowance of this much. And if I earned $100,000 a season for the next 10 years, this is how much I would have on retirement.

It was impressive. But then he said to me: 'You know what? I'm not here to convince you to sign with me. That's not what I'm about. If you're a good person, and you want someone good to look after you, I'll do it. And I'm not going to sign you to a long-term deal. If you want out, give me two weeks' notice, I'll get all your money together and we'll shake hands and call it quits.'

I signed the contract that day.

I didn't even get around to asking him the questions that any 17-year-old kid would, which were written at the bottom of the notepad I had with me. 'Can you hook me up with celebrity women?' I'd read about the managers in the NFL getting in touch with celebrity women and hooking the pairs up. 'If I was stuck in Kings Cross at 2 a.m., would you pick me up?' I never got to ask that one either. I'd already found out what I really needed to know.

Martin would fly me to Sydney to look around. We started to look for places where I could live. Our relationship was actually like father and son. We fight. It's the same with Tim really. We are so close that of course we are going to have disagreements. But half an hour later, we have invariably made up.

If I didn't have him in my corner, I don't know where I would be. I had nothing growing up, and I believe that if I didn't have him, I'd still have nothing. I find it hard to say no. If people ask me for something, I generally give them what they're after. He has had to force me to say no on occasions. Or he would step in and do so himself. I always want to help people, especially family. But he knows that one of my goals was to make sure I didn't end up with nothing. It's still written in my file. He hides my own money from me for my own good. He has secret accounts that he thinks I don't know about.

As well, there have been so many occasions when I've needed a friend more than a manager, and he has been there for me. I look up to him as if he is a father to me, and I think he looks at me like his son.

He does his job the way a manager should. But I don't see him as a manager. And I don't see him doing a job for me. I see him as a real friend.

Chapter 4

A Pub Team

ALL PREMIERSHIPS seem to end in the pub, but our journey towards the 2005 title actually began in one. Our team always had a fairly clear divide between youth and, well, experienced. 'Sheensy' had always addressed us as either the 'senior guys' or the 'young blokes'. By 2004, though, the young blokes were outnumbering the senior guys.

The core of the squad, Mark O'Neill, Corey Pearson, Ben Galea, John Skandalis and Daniel Fitzhenry, called us together and one of them said: 'Boys, let's go to the pub. Go home and tell your missus you're not going to be home until tomorrow.' So on a Monday night, after training, we all went to Tracks nightclub at Epping.

It worked wonders. I was always made to feel welcome at the club; there was never a stage when I didn't feel like I belonged at the Tigers. It might sound corny but the club has a homely feel. But that was the night when the team really started to come together. We still respected the older players. You'd never, ever, raise your voice to a senior player, not like youngsters do now.

Mark was very easy to respect. He was the captain at the time. He was a serious character. When we used to do fitness drills, I used to win much of the time because I was so light and so fit. He took me aside on one occasion and said: 'You're making us old blokes look bad — stay with the team.'

The next time we ran, Tim actually said to me: 'You'd better win this one, Benji.' Which put me in a quandary, of course. Who should I listen to? My coach or my captain? I won the drill by a mile, and Mark said to me: 'Did you not hear me the first time? Stay with the team.' There were a few other choice words thrown in. I said: 'Sheensy told me to win.' 'Who's more important,' he asked, 'Sheensy or the team?'

So before the next one, of course, Tim said to me: 'Get them again, boy.' But this time, I stayed with the team. I made sure that I let Mark cross the line before me. He came up to me, shook my hand and said: 'That was a test of respect, and you've got my respect. When you're on the field, you don't have your coach next to you. Who do you listen to?' 'You, Mark,' I replied. From then on, whatever he told me to do, I'd do.

FROM THE moment he first saw me play, as a schoolboy, I think Tim always liked me because I was different. He treated me differently, too. I'm not sure why. He treats every player differently, but he treats me way differently. When Keebra Park linked with the Tigers, and Tim became their coach, it felt like it was meant to be. I felt like we were supposed to be together as coach and player.

I trusted Tim from very early on. In 2004, when I was negotiating my future with the Tigers, or elsewhere, he said to me: 'You've just got to do what's best for you and your family. I'd love to have you here, but if you don't think it's here, you have to move on.' I stayed, of course. I would have stayed regardless, but I trusted him because of his honesty. We all did.

Tim told us if we were to have any chance of making the finals, the younger blokes would have to stand up and act like senior players. He asked us how we were going to do that. I said: 'For a start, stop calling us younger blokes.' So he told the senior players to stop calling us 'younger blokes'.

I wasn't in the subsequent meeting he had with the senior guys, but he later told me what he said. When you are young, and you try to offload and it doesn't come off, the senior guys tend to come down on you quite hard, but Tim told them to let us play our game. He told them if we were to have a good season, the young blokes were going to be the reason why. 'So let them do what they do,' he said. They let me play my role at five-eighth.

It was easy for me in '05. Scott Prince would direct the forwards around, and if I'd see something out wide and call for the ball, he'd give it to me no matter what. Halfway through the season, Robbie Farah became the starting hooker for us, and we started to form a great combination.

By that time, we were sitting eleventh; we were showing glimpses of good footy, and everyone enjoyed the way we were playing. But we were still losing games. So we sat down in the upstairs meeting room at our Concord training base and reassessed our goals.

'Okay, so what's realistic?' the coach asked. 'We are eleventh now. What should we aim for? Top eight? Does that sound realistic?' We all seemed to agree. But then Ben Galea piped up, saying: 'Why would we aim so low? Why do you want to scrape into the top eight and just be happy to make the finals?' He started pointing. 'Do you not believe in us?' he said. 'Do you not believe in this team?'

Tim told us to go out and tell the media that we were aiming for the top four. So that week, when the media came on Tuesday, Benny Galea told them we'd set a new goal: top four. I'm sure some of them were laughing at us. I'm also certain that, deep down, some of the boys in our team were laughing as well.

But not Benny Galea. Sure enough, every week, he would say to us, 'Top four boys.' We started an extras board; every week each of us had to do something difficult with someone else, then write it on the board, so the whole team could see what extra steps we were taking, whether it be extra sprinting or extra cardio. It brought us a lot closer.

IT ALSO brought results. We won two in a row, three in a row, then four in a row, and all of a sudden we were nudging the top eight. Then we played Cronulla, which was one of my personal highlights of the season. I regard it as one of the best games I've ever played.

It also included one of the best tries of the year. Princey dropped me under, and I stepped about three defenders; I went past Phil Bailey, then rounded David Peachey, threw a no-look pass to Pat Richards, who sent an inside ball to Daniel Fitzhenry. It felt amazing.

It gave me a lot of confidence to start doing a lot more. After that game, I was doing flick passes. I was throwing everything you can think of. I was getting all my tricks out. I was so young and so naive and I wanted to try everything. I was loving it. It was like we were playing in the park. Then all of a sudden we had hit eight wins in a row, and fourth place.

We were comfortably going to make the finals, so we were already making history for the club. Then we lost our last two games of the regular season, against Melbourne in Melbourne and Penrith at Homebush. Everyone wrote us off again. Everyone, I should say, except our own supporters. I'll never forget the way they turned up to our first training session of the finals. Hundreds of people watched us train at Concord. It felt like we were already in the grand final.

Funnily enough, on that first weekend of the finals, we played the team we would ultimately play in the decider, North Queensland, on a Friday night at Homebush. I was thinking: 'How good is this?' I couldn't believe we were there. I don't think anyone could. Tim told us to just do our best. 'We've made it this far,' he told us. 'We've already broken records.' I don't think he expected us to get as far as we did.

In the dressing room on the night of that first final, I looked around and, for the first time that year, noticed that everyone was very serious. Usually, there was a bit of laughing and joking in our dressing room, but not on this occasion. I could tell we were ready to play. And so it proved. We won 50–4.

It was such a buzz. After the game, we were hugging, high-fiving — like we'd won the whole comp. Sure enough, the fans turned up in their droves again. We were getting mobbed in the street. I couldn't go shopping at the supermarket. Tigers fans were stopping me everywhere I went. I saw Tigers flags in the street and on cars. It was crazy, but it was a great feeling. People were talking about the style of football we were playing, just shifting the ball around; we didn't have the biggest forward pack, but we had one of the greatest forward packs I've played with in terms of heart and ability, guys like Mark O'Neill and John Skandalis, who had never played a final up to that point. Just to have them there was a buzz.

We played Brisbane next, at the Sydney Football Stadium. Even though they had lost on the first weekend, we weren't really expected to beat them. The coach had asked us if we wanted to go into camp for a few days. We told him we'd gotten that far by doing one routine, so we might as well stick to it. The night before we played the Cowboys, Robbie Farah and I had stayed at Dene Halatau's place, with his mum and his sister at North Parramatta. We ate there and just relaxed together — we'd sing, play cards, whatever we felt like doing. And then we drove to the game the next day. We decided to do the same again before the Broncos game.

When you're around other boys you tend to forget about the football. I've always been fairly relaxed, while the other two could be tense. I tried to lighten up the mood with a joke, relax them a bit. I was just happy to be there; if we won or lost it didn't seem to matter, although obviously I desperately wanted to win.

As we were driving to the ground, I was stunned by the sheer number of people heading down Cleveland Street towards the Moore Park precinct; cars filled with Tigers jerseys, flags hanging out the windows, people walking up the street quicker than the traffic. We were in Dene's silver Mitsubishi Lancer, and soon enough some people started noticing us. They were banging on the windows, high-fiving us, asking us for photos . . . I thought we were going to be late for the game, but then some of the cars started moving out of the way for us. I've never felt so pumped up; every car had jerseys inside and then streamers or flags outside. We felt like we were kings. At the start of that season, I knew many of the faces at our home games, but by the end of it, I saw so many new people, some who might have stopped supporting the club after the merger. The numbers got me. I don't know where they'd come from, or where they'd been, but there was a sea of black and orange that night.

During the finals, the coach wanted us to warm up for games on the field, so we could get a feeling for the atmosphere. When you call the plays, you need to get used to hearing it among so much noise. Heading out for our warm-up against the Broncos gave me a feeling I'd never experienced. We all started high-fiving each other. 'How good is this?' we were saying.

We went back into the sheds, and the coach gave his speech. 'Look, boys,' he said, 'no one really expected us to get this far, whatever happens happens. There are no expectations, I am proud of you for getting this far.' I looked at Brett Hodgson, and he said: 'We could do something special this year.'

Brisbane had us under the pump for 25 minutes. They were camped on our tryline. They were making breaks everywhere; Tonie Carroll, Darren Lockyer . . . but our scramble defence was phenomenal. When Carroll made a break, I chased him down from my wing, where I was defending. We were outnumbered. They shifted, and when Darren Smith turned the ball back inside for Brad Thorn, I sprinted in from the marker, and took an intercept. I raced 90 metres and by the time I reached the tryline I was so tired that I tripped over it.

Mark O'Neill was playing his first game after an elbow injury, and soon after halftime, he threw the biggest dummy I'd seen and scored his first try of the year. We sprinted in from everywhere to congratulate him. I ran in from the other side of the field; it was his first finals appearance and we mobbed him. We ended up winning quite comfortably. We went back into the sheds after the game and we still couldn't believe what had happened. What we did know is we were playing St George Illawarra, who had the weekend off.

The Dragons were the favourites in just about everyone's eyes but ours. But this was our chance — win and we're in a grand final. They had a wonderful team; Mark Gasnier, Matt Cooper, Trent Barrett, all in their prime. But they also had the pressure. That was the point that Tim made. He told us all the pressure was on them. Still, it was difficult not to feel any. We'd gone from being fairly relaxed to stressing out a little. We were one game away from a grand final, after all. Everyone was on edge. But we were in good form. I remember training and just realising how everything was running like clockwork. I had the feeling that every time I touched the ball, something good was going to happen.

WE FOLLOWED the 'if you find a good thing, stick to it' rule. We didn't go into camp, preferring to have some team lunches during the week. As before, I stayed with Dene the night before we played. That night, Robbie said to us: 'Let's write a poem.' It was about our season, getting to the grand final. It took about an hour to write it. We were in the lounge room, just bored, I guess. Robbie was on the computer typing it up. Dene and I would come up with rhyming words. 'What's a word that rhymes with "fingers"?' Robbie would say. It's a pretty cool poem. I remember that night like it was yesterday.

Again, we travelled to the Sydney Football Stadium in Dene's silver car. We left earlier, but it made little difference; the traffic was worse this time and, again, the supporters spotted us in our awful club purple shirts and leather jackets, and we needed a security escort from the car park.

I thought the St George Illawarra fans might outnumber our supporters, but I saw black, white and orange everywhere I looked. We all went out and had a look at the field. It was a perfect night for football.

A PUB TEAM

After Tim spoke, telling us again how proud he was that we had gone as far as we had, he left the dressing room, and we spoke among ourselves. It was mostly Brett Hodgson and Scott Prince doing the talking. The gist of it was that we shouldn't worry about what everyone else thought. *We can do this. Why not go one more step?* We were so pumped up.

The cheer when we ran out was just about the loudest I have heard. There was plenty of red and white in the crowd, but the Tigers supporters still dominated them in terms of noise, I thought. I was thinking to myself, 'Incredible. I'm 20 years old, and one step away from a grand final.' In among the throng was a lot of my family. I think they came over because they were worried we might not make it any further. They thought they'd better get over to see this while they had a chance.

But we gave ourselves every chance to win that game. We were quietly confident we could upset them and we knew the pressure was on them. We were just a young group of guys throwing the ball.

Just before the game, Tim had picked that particular time to tell me he had a new scrum play. He said: 'If we get a scrum, this is what I want you to do.' I said: 'You're telling me now?' He said: 'Yeah, you'll be right. Just tell Hodgo [Brett Hodgson] and Shane Elford.' I said: 'What about rest of the team?' 'No, that's all,' he replied. So I told Hodgo and Shane, and like me they expressed their doubts. Sure enough, about two minutes in, the Dragons dropped the ball in their own half. I looked at Hodgo. We realised we'd better do it. Tim was calling it from the sideline. The way the move worked, Hodgo would get the ball off the scrum, drop the blind-side centre under him. Shane is lead runner for me and I'd sweep out the back on Mark Gasnier, because he always seemed to come up. So we ran it. Brett was at first-receiver from the scrum, and I was a bit wider. Shane was outside me, but he ran a block run and I swept out the back. Brett dummied to the man coming under. Sure enough, Mark Gasnier came in and it was too late for him to recover. Colin Best was in front of me and I knew if I threw a dummy he'd stick on his winger. I dummied and I scored in the corner. I threw the ball in the air. Pat Richards ran over and I jumped on him. He was holding me up with my legs wrapped around his waist, and my hand in the air. I looked over to the sideline to see Tim just nodding. As I walked back to halfway he said: 'I told you.'

It was the toughest, most physical game I'd played to date. The Dragons never gave up, fought all the way. I regard it as one of the greatest games I've played in, just knowing how hard we had worked. Pat Richards had gone off with an ankle injury. The Dragons threw everything at us late in the game. Scott Prince covered back for a grubber, they shifted to Gasnier and Shane Elford covered him for me. They put another grubber through and Hodgo ran it dead with 25 seconds left. I looked around and all the Tigers fans were going mad. I looked at Skando and Mark O'Neill. They went to each other, cuddled and got teary. We put our grand final T-shirts on, and we felt like we'd already won the thing. We were doing laps around the field. It was the most unbelievable feeling to know we had made the grand final. I looked up in the stands as I walked off and saw my family. They were crying. I started crying.

In the dressing room, the coach told us: 'We're here, so we may as well go one more step.' We all met up the next day, at Paul Whatuira's place, to watch the second preliminary final. We couldn't believe Parramatta lost to the Cowboys, but we didn't care who we played. All we cared about was being there.

A PUB TEAM

Beyond all expectations

Lost for words as I try to comprehend how far we have come as the journey nears its end.
We started months ago, little did we expect, that we'd be sitting here today, allowing ourselves to reflect.
'Too young and too small', no one gave us a chance.
They've all changed their minds now, 80 minutes from our grand final dance.
A joy to watch, the crowds come flocking; on the door of greatness we are now knocking.
We must hold our nerves, can't let this opportunity slip through our fingers,
Best of mates we are, creating history together lingers.
We've waited so long for success to come our way, two proud clubs merged together we stand here today.
Impatiently we've waited so long for tomorrow to come around, but it will be worth it as we run onto the hallowed ground.
The fans will cheer loud, maybe even a tear in the eye; because the team that they love is finally flying high.
If it comes to an end there still will be celebrations, because this youthful team of mates has achieved beyond all expectations.
So the fairytale continues for at least another day, with only two more opponents standing in our way.
One more down tomorrow, one more to go, the nation will stand still, because this team will put on a show.
A fairytale ending befits this fairytale story, one that we only dream of, one that ends in glory!

Robbie Farah (with a little help from Benji Marshall and Dene Halatau)

23 September 2005

Chapter 5

One Week of All Time

THE GREATEST week of my life began like any other. But clearly it wasn't. Training at 10 a.m. at Concord Oval. What was a bit different was the fact that by 9 a.m. the place was filled with life. Cars outside the ground and people everywhere. They were cheering as I drove in.

The players were still hugging and high-fiving when we arrived. It was as if we were kids again. I guess many of us were, really. Tim told us the week was going to be a distracting one: promos, media, packed training sessions, the grand-final breakfast. As we ran out for our first training session of the week, the supporters started crowding the tunnel at Concord. I must admit, I thought to myself: 'Why not try and get a big cheer here?' I said to Daniel Fitzhenry: 'Let's go out together, man.' So we put our arms around each other and walked out. There would have been a couple of thousand people there. It gave us a big buzz. It was the most fun you could have at a training session.

On the Wednesday night of grand-final week, we went into camp together. We had the traditional breakfast the next morning, but we still had a bit of fun on Wednesday night, playing poker together at the hotel. I'd never been to a grand-final breakfast, so I didn't know what to expect. The club had ordered us some new clothes — it was a relief to get out of the purple shirt and leather jacket ensemble. It was all a bit overwhelming, though. I was starting to get sick of the cameras.

At the breakfast, I saw Johnathan Thurston with his own hand-held camera, filming the whole event. Matty Bowen was doing the same. It was strange for me. You sit up on the front table and look out at everyone, while they all stare at you. I had to answer a few questions on stage. Tim had already given us a spiel. 'Don't give the Cowboys any ammunition,' he'd said. So I was trying to be careful what I said. I was only 20 years old at the time and I thought I handled it quite well.

We had another training session immediately after the breakfast. Pat Richards had been cleared of a broken ankle, and he was spending a lot of time in a hyperbaric chamber in an attempt to play. But, at that stage, it was still highly unlikely he was going to. We all hung out together for a lot of the week. The whole experience brought us closer together.

We had the Friday off and we were able to break camp and spend time with family. I had to head home to start organising some extra mattresses. I had about 30 people staying in my three-bedroom apartment at Westmead, which takes some doing. My grandfather was coming over — he was getting on a plane for the first time to watch me play. I had to organise about 90 tickets for the game. Mick and Annalie, their kids Troy, Nicola and Paula, my uncles John, Phil and Luke. My uncle Bensy, who lived on the sixth floor of the same apartment block, was taking his wife, Michelle, and their son Michael. He and his family had needed a change and decided to come to Australia. Michael was becoming a teenager, and they wanted to get him to school in Sydney. Bensy looked after me, too. We had a close relationship. He was like my father. He was there for me whether he was giving me a lift in his car or sharing a beer with me. He never told me I had a bad game or criticised me. It was good to share a lot of the week with him.

Some of my other cousins were there as well: Linda, Mark, Marshall, Rhys and Paul. My Uncle John brought some mates, Woody and Leon, who were like uncles to me. Bensy cooked. He always did for our family barbecues. We mucked around, played cards, chilled out and talked. A lot of my family had never seen a game live and I was excited that they were able to see this one. It was an unbelievable night. It gave me a release from the pressure of the week. It was good to just chill out. I slept on the floor. My family wanted me to sleep in my own bed, but I wanted to sleep on the floor like everyone else. It was just how we did it. I did have a mattress.

WE HAD trained all week thinking that Pat Richards was not going to play. Before our final training session, on the Saturday, he was about 50–50. He received a number of painkilling injections just to have a run that day.

He completed a fitness test before we trained, unbeknown to the rest of us. I was putting on my boots when he came into the dressing room, sweating, with the physio and the doctor alongside him. He had his head down, and we all felt shattered for him. He was limping, and he looked devastated. We all went quiet, then he said: 'I'm in.' We looked at the doctor, who confirmed it. We all cheered and hugged him. We all felt bad for Shannon McDonnell, who had trained in Pat's place all week, but Patty was instrumental in getting us to the grand final. It would have been awful for him to miss out. He would have spent several hours a day in the hyperbaric chamber, icing the ankle at other times, day and night. I don't think he would have slept much that week. He didn't train with us, didn't attend the breakfast. He quietly did all the hard work while the rest of us were resigned to the fact he would not be playing.

The news gave us a massive boost for the training session. It was the best training session of the week; it was smooth, and everything went to plan. We felt confident. We felt ready.

I WAS still 20, so this was around the time when a lot of my mates were turning 21. It just so happened that the night before the grand final, one of my best friends was celebrating his. I wasn't going to miss it.

Woody grew up with me in Whakatane. I knew I couldn't stay for long, but I wanted to be there to have a feed with him and give him a haka. I didn't tell any of my teammates that I was going because they all prepare differently and they might have raised an eyebrow. I knew I'd be able to handle it. I relaxed with my family in the afternoon and then joined them at Woody's twenty-first, at the Collector Hotel in Parramatta.

Half the pub was closed off for the party and the other half was open for the regulars. Many of them couldn't believe I was in there. I had a feed, drank water, waited until we had done the haka for Woody and by 11 p.m. I thought I'd better leave. I was staying, again, at Dene's house, and all night he and Robbie had been phoning me, stressing out. 'Where are you, man?' they'd say. 'We've got a grand final tomorrow.' I was hungry on my way back, and felt like a couple of cheeseburgers, so I phoned the two of them and asked them if they wanted some McDonald's. They told me I wasn't getting McDonald's. I told them I was.

I bought a large Big Mac meal and four cheeseburgers, just

in case the other boys felt like one. I walked into Dene's house carrying a big brown McDonald's bag and slurping on a Coke, and they blew up at me. 'What are you doing?' they yelled. 'We've got to play tomorrow.' I said: 'It's only Maccas.'

I didn't know any different back then. To me that was normal. I ate my Big Mac meal, and they didn't want the cheeseburgers so I gulped down two of them.

By about 1 a.m. we thought we'd get some sleep. I slept in Dene's lounge, as I had done over the last four weeks. Tim had asked us if we wanted to stay in camp on match eve, but the entire team wanted to stick to the same routine. It had got us that far. Why change it? Many of us were superstitious at that age. We thought any change would bring everything undone.

Dene reckoned he didn't get much sleep. Neither did Robbie. I slept like a baby. It must have been the burgers. They were both up early, but I slept in for a while longer. I could tell they were nervous.

WE WERE due to meet at the Novotel, a hotel in the Homebush precinct, about 2 p.m. The club had booked us rooms for the afternoon, so we could have lunch as a team and then have a sleep, or just relax before the game.

I went to each room trying to find someone to talk to. Mark O'Neill and Ben Galea were both crashed out. The only person I could find who wasn't asleep was Liam Fulton. Bryce Gibbs was in his room trying to sleep, and Liam and I were trying to crack jokes and make prank calls. Gibbo had to find my room so he could get some sleep. Some people need to be serious before games; some play better when they are relaxed. I've learnt to stay away from the serious ones because if you try to joke with them they'll knock you out.

Before we knew it, we had to get our team uniforms on. I always used to try to watch a bit of the earlier game, but on this occasion I didn't. Tim had put together all the tries and good plays from the year on a video projector. We sat and watched all the good things we'd done throughout the year. It really pumped us up to see all the great tries we had scored.

I like to get ready last. I had never heard a dressing room so quiet. I looked at Liam and he was motioning to me to be quiet. I went over to him and we had a bit of a laugh. All the boys looked at us, like they couldn't believe what we were doing. Brett Hodgson joined us. We'd gotten that far by being who we were. There was no point trying to change things by getting all serious.

In '05, I always put my left sock on before my left shoe, and then my right sock and boot. I also wore the same underpants every week. Darren Lockyer had said he used to do it so I copied him. It seemed to work for him and I reckon it did for me, too. Suddenly I realised that I was putting my right sock on before my left boot. I had to quickly take it off and put my left shoe on. I had a photograph of my family — me, my mum and my brothers — which I'd always look at before games. I attached it to my little booth in the dressing room. I looked at that for a while, and then I started to get nervous. It was the first time I'd really experienced butterflies. I told the coach I was a little nervous and he said: 'Butterflies are good.' I took his word for it. We'd been warming up on the field every week, but on this occasion, we weren't allowed to. We had to warm up inside, which felt a little weird. A couple of passes didn't stick . . . everyone was a little on edge. I thought: 'I'm going to pump things up.' I started talking as much as I could. 'Let's go . . . come on' — I always had the biggest mouth, even though I was still young.

Running the ball against the Rabbitohs at the Sydney Football Stadium on 21 March 2004.

Action Photographics

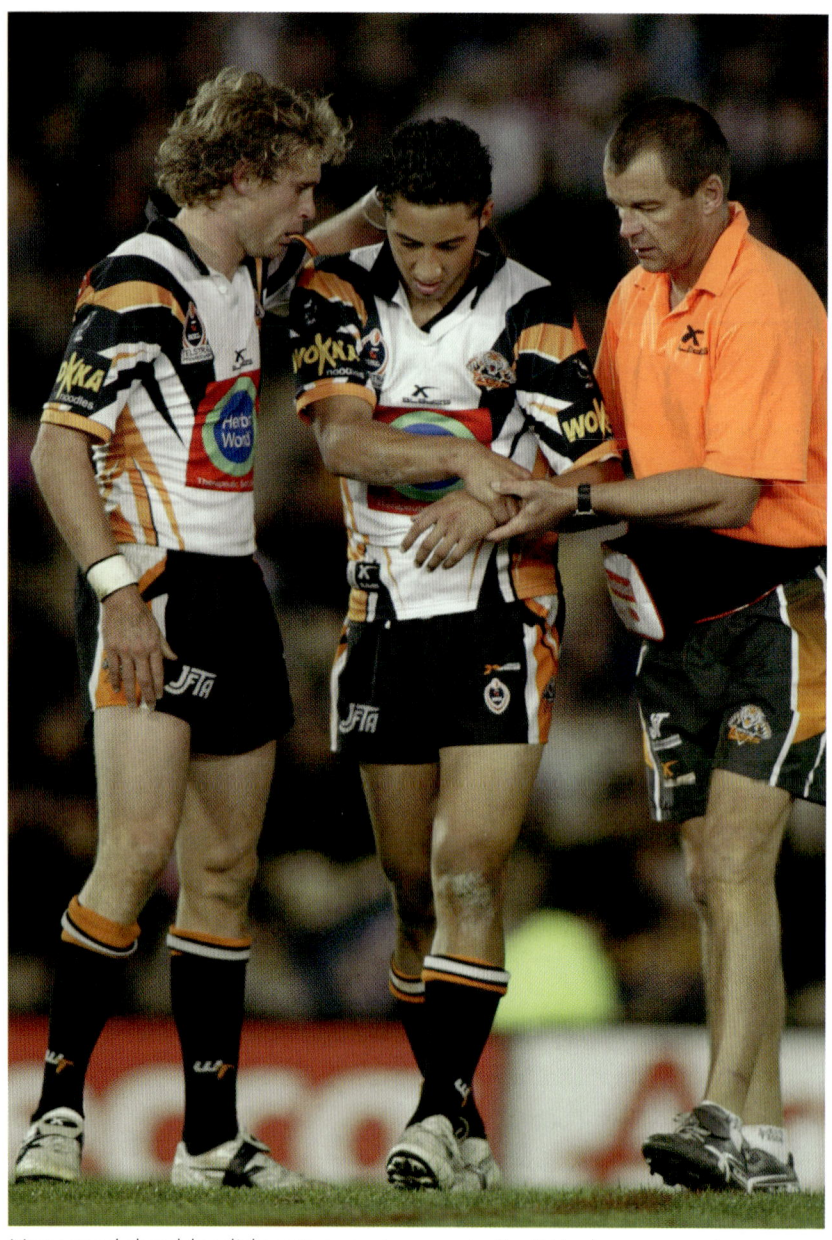

My second shoulder dislocation; my teammate Brett Hodgson consoles me as I'm helped off against Melbourne Storm at Olympic Park on 5 June 2004. I'd come off second best tackling Steve Bell. I had my first reconstruction a few days later.

Above and below: My moment in the 2005 grand final; I skip past North Queensland's Matt Sing, before a flick to Pat Richards. He did incredibly well to catch it.

Action Photographics

I'm not sure what Norm Provan and Arthur Summons are saying to each other but I'm trying to find out.

Above: The best shower I've ever had; celebrating the grand final win with my teammates.

Left: My brother, Jordan, and me on the lap of honour. After the grand final, I played an impromptu game of touch footy with both my brothers.

One of the freakiest things I've done: a no-look pass to Michael Crockett to beat the Dragons at the Olympic Stadium at Homebush in round one, 2006. Unbeknown to me I had a broken cheekbone.

Action Photographics

We always fight; Scott Prince giving me some advice against Manly, 9 June 2006.

Doherty Collection

With Tigers teammates Bronson Harrison (left) and Scott Prince (right).

On the charge, with Todd Payten right behind me, against North Queensland on 7 April 2006.

Against the Panthers at Penrith, 24 June 2006 . . .

. . . Not long after, I suffered another shoulder dislocation. My season is over.

All of a sudden we were called to line up in the tunnel. Someone at the front — I'm still not sure who it was — yelled out 'Brothers!' and then 'Brothers for life!' It spread through the whole team. We could hear our trainer Bryan Hyder, in the background, saying, 'No regrets.' Most of us giggled. Bryan said that every week. Here we were yelling 'Brothers', and in the background there was this lone voice saying, 'No regrets'. *We're trying to be serious here, Bryan. We've got a grand final to play.*

Chapter 6

Grand Occasion

I KNEW where my family was sitting. They were way up in the nosebleed section. I had already checked their seats on the stadium map on the Internet. I looked up during the national anthem and I could see them all standing there. I couldn't really see the emotion on their faces but I squinted to see anyway. I got a bit teary myself as I did so.

The week had gone like clockwork but the match itself did not follow the plan. In 14 of our previous 20 matches, we'd scored first, and we'd prided ourselves on being able to get out of the blocks quicker than our opponents. But Matt Bowen, the Cowboys fullback, scored first in the grand final and we immediately dropped our heads. We hadn't been in that position many times before so we didn't really know how to handle it. We huddled behind the tryline and a few of the guys spoke. We knew we were better than that. 'No more tries,' we said to each other.

Bryce Gibbs came on and with his first touch of the ball scored off a Cowboys error. Scott Prince had put a kick up and Paul Bowman tried to offload the ball in-goal to Bowen. It went straight to ground and Bryce, who hadn't scored all year, came through and planted his big arm on the ball. Things started to go our way, but it was still a tough contest.

Pat Richards was finding it especially so. Just before halftime, he said to me: 'Bagz, my leg's hurting, man, I'm going to have to go off soon.' I told him to just hang in there and wait until halftime. I was defending on the wing, with Pat positioned inside me. I dropped back on the last tackle as Johnathan Thurston kicked down the short side. Our fullback Brett Hodgson picked it up, and as he did so I thought I'd wrap around him. Travis Norton tried to smash Hodgo but he still got the ball away to me. Everything just opened up. It was like it was meant to be. Thurston had fallen when he kicked the ball so he was out of the chasing line, so when Brett sent me the ball, a big hole had opened up for me to run through. Usually, I tried to step my way through the kick-chase but I just went for the gap.

By the time Thurston got back into the line, I had already gotten past him. Matt Sing couldn't get me, neither could David Faiumu. The next thing I knew, I only had Bowen in front of me. Usually, I'd try to step him, but on this occasion I thought I'd try something different. I'm sure he thought I was going to step, so I tried a goose step. It didn't work; he was still coming for me.

I was looking towards the corner where I was trying to get to, and out of my left eye, I could see someone flying up the sideline. I made out the goatee and figured it was Pat Richards. I knew Bowen was going to bundle me over the sideline, so I had to think of something quick. I was going to kick ahead but I had a quick look at Pat and realised he was on his own.

I did not plan it. I really don't know how it happened. Instinct took over, and I flicked it out the back. Pat took it well, and then put one of the biggest fends I'd seen in my life on Rod Jensen, straight in the face, and he scored in the corner.

I couldn't believe what had happened. I was stunned. Patty scored the try, but all the boys came running for me. I didn't realise what I'd actually done. It all happened so quickly. I watched it on the replay and thought: 'Holy hell, I flicked it.' Patty gave me a big hug and said: 'Thanks, man, I needed that.' He told me he had to go off because his leg was hurting so much. I could tell it was, because he was limping. He was in pain, but he'd played through it.

For him to be there and catch that ball was amazing. For him to play was amazing. He deserves a lot of credit for that try. If he hadn't played on it might not have happened. Not every winger would have seen the break and followed me in like he did.

WE WERE still fairly pumped up at halftime. I looked at Scott Prince and we said: 'We can do this, let's do something special.' Hodgo came over and we had this three-way hug. We used to call ourselves the tripod back then.

We scored first in the second half, through Anthony Laffranchi, which gave us an 18–6 lead. Then the Cowboys came back at us again, Travis Norton scoring off a Thurston flick pass. Daniel Fitzhenry scored in the corner and suddenly we were up by a relatively comfortable margin.

But when the Cowboys want to throw the ball around, they can do anything. With about two minutes to go, they scored a great try. Thurston and Bowen were both involved and Matt Sing scored. Suddenly, we lost a bit of hope. Our heads were down and we were nervous. Josh Hannay needed to kick the conversion from about 15 metres in from touch to keep them in the game. With the clock ticking, he tried to rush the kick, and he missed it. We were eight points ahead.

The Cowboys lost the ball as they threw it around at the death. And we found ourselves on the attack in the final moments. Hodgo went to the line and Toddy Payten started pointing at the posts for a kick — a big forward pointing at the posts for a kick! But he's smart, Todd. He knew Matty Bowen had just made a tackle on Paul Whatuira and was out of position. There was no fullback. Liam and Toddy both charged through and I think Toddy pushed Liam out of the way to score. We all stacked on Toddy and I remember running around the crowd, high-fiving people. Hodgo kicked the goal. Game over. I just went quiet. I went to a different planet. I couldn't believe what had just happened. I saw Thurston and Bowen sitting on the ground and, knowing how shattered I would be in their position, I walked over and shook their hands first, while all my teammates hugged and high-fived each other. I said: 'Unlucky, you had a great season, you did well to be here.' Johnathan was crying. I just thought it was what I had to do.

I ran over to my team. I was giving them all hugs, and Mark O'Neill kissed me on the head, saying: 'I love you, brothers for life.' Tim squeezed me like I'd never been squeezed in my life. The enormity of it had not sunk in by then. It felt surreal more than anything. I saw my little brothers in the crowd. I grabbed a ball and said: 'This is for you. If it wasn't for you, I wouldn't be here. I'm doing this for you.' I started playing a bit of touch footy with them on the field, while the rest of the team began a lap of honour. I ended up taking them on the lap of honour, too. They were quite young, Jordan 13 and Jeremy maybe 10. They loved being there, high-fiving the crowd. I even saw my hairdresser on the lap of honour, and gave him a big hug.

THE ONE downer was that I couldn't see the rest of my family. I wanted them to be a part of it, and it made me a bit emotional. I went back down the tunnel, taking my brothers with me, as we waited for Tim to give us a speech. As we waited, the Channel Seven reporter Pat Molihan approached me with his camera and told me he'd found my family. I said: 'What?' They were all upstairs, he told me.

I walked up there, without a shirt, with just my shorts, socks and the premiership ring on, and I saw them all waiting there for me, at the bottom of the big circular walkway at the entrance to the Homebush stadium. I gave Mum a kiss, then saw my grandfather, who was crying, and I gave him a hug. He said: 'In all my life, this is the proudest I've ever been.' I just lost it. I started crying, too. And I couldn't stop. My grandfather is a legendary figure around Whakatane. Any man who can have that many kids and keep track of them is doing rather well! I can't keep track of them all. Most of what we do now as a family revolves around him. It was so important to have him there. He's done a lot of things, he's had a lot of kids — and grandkids — but for him to say he was the proudest he'd been . . . well, it meant a lot to me that it meant so much to him. I thought about what he said for years.

Where I'm from, it's tradition to do a haka on special occasions, whether it be someone's birthday, or funeral, or even if something good happens to someone. I'd never had a haka done for me, and as I turned around, my little brothers, my uncles and Woody started busting out our local haka. I was lost for words. When they finished, I shook everyone's hand, gave everyone a cuddle and said: 'See you at the leagues club.'

TIM ACTUALLY told us afterwards he thought we were going to bundle out in the semis. But he still came prepared for victory. He brought out a cigar, lit it up, then started skolling some beer and champagne. I don't know if you are allowed to smoke in the Homebush dressing rooms but we did. We all did. Tim reckoned it was an expensive cigar, but by the time it got to me it was wet and disgusting. I'd never smoked in my life, so I wrapped my lips around it and . . . I thought to myself, 'I don't care what he says, I'm not sucking on this cigar.' So I pretended to, skolled some of the champagne, and posed for a photograph with the Prime Minister, John Howard. Just another day really.

Tim thanked everyone, all the staff and players, and tried to emphasise what we'd achieved. He said we wouldn't really know what it meant until later on in our careers. He was right, too. It took me a while to really understand what it meant to a lot of the supporters. I was so young. I probably didn't really appreciate it until a year later. I hadn't been around the club for that long, so I didn't really know what it meant. I was just celebrating.

We didn't want to leave the sheds. All the media came in. The room was just full of people; it was just crazy. The coach told us to 'lap it up'. We got dressed into black 'Wests Tigers Premiers' shirts. There was a bus waiting for us at the stadium, to take us to the Wests Ashfield Leagues Club. We were driven out from underneath the stadium, and there was a wall of fans to greet us and see us off. We told the driver to drive slowly. The supporters were banging on the windows and we were jumping up and down. It didn't take long for the smell of alcohol to overpower the bus.

We arrived at the leagues club to the sight of a queue of people trying to get in. But the leagues club was already full inside. I ripped the sleeves off my shirt and made a headband. We were told to have something to eat. *It's going to be a long night.* 'Yeah, of course it is, but eating is cheating.' We did have a bit of food, but we wanted to get on stage in the auditorium.

GRAND OCCASION

We walked out with the trophy and they lifted the roof off. A few of us got to talk and say thanks to the fans: Tim, Scott Prince. Then they gave me the microphone. I had had a bit to drink by that stage, so I started belting out 'We are the Champions'. The supporters started singing, too, and then a few of the boys started crowd surfing. But we had to get to Balmain Leagues Club, so they snuck us out the back door. A couple of people tried to jump on the bus and had to be forced off.

Our manager stood up and told us that part of Victoria Road had to be closed. We turned into it and there were people all the way down to the Iron Cove Bridge. Victoria Road was full of supporters, so was Darling Street. A path had to be cleared so we could make our way to the entrance. We were each given a bottle of champagne after we made our way inside. We were led to a balcony roof, where we shook the champagne bottles and sprayed it. I thought it was a waste so I skolled some of it. We all went upstairs, for a function with family and friends. We walked through the door and they all came running to meet us.

Steve Noyce, the club boss, told us there was an open bar tab, so we had a drink and enjoyed each other's company. It was actually quite hard to see the other boys, because everyone had so many family and friends. I did find enough time with Dene Halatau to make a pact that we wouldn't sleep for two days. My Uncle Phil kept telling me, 'It's my shout', when the beers were free. At about 3 a.m., Chris Heighington's father had to take him home. He had already poured a glass of beer over Paul Sironen's head, after which a few of us took him into a back room to calm down a bit. He asked for a vodka, so I gave him a glass of water with ice in it. We told his dad to have him back to the bus by 9.30 the next morning.

I had a couple of my best mates there, Jamie Stowe, who

plays touch football for Australia, and Adam Lollback. Most of my family had gone home by this stage. I went for a walk and caught Dean trying to catch some sleep under a table. I said: 'Hey what are you doing here?' 'Yeah, you got me,' he said. I lay next to him and we had about an hour's sleep. We went back downstairs and my Uncle Phil was asleep on the bar. I threw a glass of water in his face.

WE ALL had to be on the bus at 9.30 a.m. All the players and some extras, too. There were a couple of people I didn't even know, so I smuggled a couple of my mates on as well. We were too pumped to sleep.

The plan was to head to Campbelltown Stadium, before bussing off to Leichhardt Oval. As we got to Campbelltown, the adrenalin was wearing off and we all started to feel the bumps and bruises from the game. They never really appear until the next day. I was limping, and my shoulder was the sorest it had been for a long time. I had actually injured it in the grand final. I felt it slip just before halftime but I stayed on the field. I wouldn't have been able to play the next week. I reckon I would have needed six weeks out, either that or go under the knife immediately. I had known that there was always a chance of that happening, and I was just fortunate it happened in the final game of the year. Having said that, I played the grand final differently, defended differently, knowing there was no next week. It was going to be the end of the season regardless of the result. I defended three-in at times and I was putting everything into tackles. I still can't believe I played that whole year. I played every game except the first round, and by the end of it all I was struggling to sign autographs.

We were all sore, though. We'd all put everything into it. None of this seemed to worry Brett Hodgson, who poured a bottle of Pepsi on Tim's head after they got off the bus at Campbelltown Stadium. Tim wrestled him and told him not to do it again. I am almost certain he was very serious.

We were lined up in the tunnel and called onto the field one by one. We walked out to big cheers from the crowd. We signed autographs and made our way back to the bus. Hodgo let Tim get on first, then proceeded to pour another bottle of Pepsi on his head. I rarely saw Sheensy become furious, even after a bad game. But he was not exactly bubbly even with a head covered in fizzy drink. He chased Hodgo. But Brett was too quick. We were all having so much fun.

There seemed to be even more people at Leichhardt. Some supporters already had premiership tattoos, and it was clear we weren't the only people to have had a big night out. We soldiered on. We went back to the leagues club, where Noycey put on another tab for us upstairs. That night, the enormity of what we'd done started to sink in, in part because we were all tired and emotional. For me, seeing what it meant to blokes like Mark O'Neill and John Skandalis was the clincher. They'd never made a final before, let alone a grand final. It meant so much to me to see them win, knowing how hard they had worked. I saw genuine tears when they put on their premiership rings. Just seeing them experience that before they retired . . . some people don't even make a grand final, let alone win one. They could have played their entire careers without playing a final.

Everyone went home that night and caught up on some sleep. We went to a terrible Irish pub on Tuesday night. Wednesday night was Benny Galea's buck's night. We met at the Epping Hotel at lunchtime. If you arrived after midday you had to drink some port. We dressed up. I went as a boxer: I had the shorts, no shirt, and I'd drawn abs with a Texta. Daniel Fitzhenry went as Robin, Skando as Batman. After dinner, we all went to the nightclub downstairs, Tracks, the very same venue we had flocked to more than a year earlier as we made a pact to become more of a close-knit team. It was always great on a Wednesday night, but it was something else the Wednesday night after the first Sunday in October. I started trying these rock 'n' roll dance moves with some girls, picking them up and dipping them; one was so tall that, when I threw her up, her head put a hole in the ceiling. She was a bit stunned. We had to get her into a cab with her friends.

On Thursday, a group of us took my mate's boat to Nick's Seafood at Darling Harbour and ordered a massive seafood platter. We were sitting on the harbour, drinking beers. We turned the laptop on and watched the game. It was the first time I'd seen it. We made a rule; every time you did something good in the game, you had to skoll. Something bad — two skolls. It was a great day. We later walked up to the Three Wise Monkeys on George Street, before heading to the Greenwood Hotel at North Sydney.

On Friday morning, someone received a phone call from Terry Hill, asking us to come to Gosford. He had a share in a bar there called Iguana Joe's. So Robbie Farah, Chris Heighington, Paul Whatuira, Dene Halatau, two of my touch football mates, Jamie Stowe and Mark Hannould, and I made our way up the F3 to the Central Coast. Stowie was the designated driver. We arrived at Terry's place, had a few beers there, before he took us over to the bar by boat.

He told us to order what we wanted. So I asked for lobster. When we finished dinner we made our way to the nightclub area. By now the word had obviously spread that a few of us might be there, so there were a heap of Tigers fans. They asked us up onto the stage, naming the boys who were there. We told them that Mark was Ray Cashmere and Stowie was Brett Hodgson. Stowie is captain of the Australian touch team, and Mark is a police officer who used to be the manager of the Wests team I played for. They haven't missed a Mad Monday since the 2005 one. Mark looks a bit like Ray, and Stowie is a skinny little dude who has a resemblance to Hodgo. Everyone was so drunk they had no idea — I think. We had a great night there.

On Saturday, though, we had to be back in Sydney for Ben Galea's wedding, at a beautiful place on the water at Drummoyne. I had no suit so I had to put on one that Stowie had. It was a few sizes too small. I almost fell asleep at the reception, and I later went back to Stowie's place to crash.

I WAS lying in bed, struggling a bit, when Stowie woke me up. 'I can't do it man,' I told him. He said to me: 'We've just won the comp.' I said: 'You didn't win it.' He said: 'I'm Brett Hodgson.' So we got up on Sunday morning and headed to the Coogee Bay Hotel. It was an amazing day. Hot, beachside; we were just relaxing in shorts and thongs and having a good time.

We were still celebrating on Monday night, more than a week after the game. We went to Scubar, which was good because in among all the backpackers we were rather incognito, just enjoying each other's company. I remember hugging Skando. 'I love you man,' we'd tell each other. 'We've done it.' I never paid for a drink all week and I never took the ring off. We ended up in a pub in Balmain. Tim had to drag me out of there. 'You've got surgery tomorrow.' It was a sobering thought, and I probably needed reminding.

Scott Prince

I HAD seen a bit of Benji by the time I joined him at the Tigers. I saw the steps he was producing, and I thought, 'This must have been the kid Tim keeps talking about.' He looked a freakish talent. Those first occasions I saw him, he hardly passed the ball, but his running game was incredible. I had played touch football, coming through the juniors, and I could tell straight away that he was a touch footballer. He had raw, untapped talent; by then, he still hadn't played much rugby league.

Benji had arrived at the club a year before I did. I had come from the Broncos, having never really wanted to go to Sydney. Tim Sheens had given me the opportunity to play in the NRL with North Queensland, and the fact that he also spoke so highly of the young batch of players coming through drew me to the Wests Tigers.

The club had been through something of an overhaul. Tim had signed me, Scott Sattler, Brett Hodgson, Pat Richards, Todd Payten and Shane Elford, among others. I walked in, at the end of 2003, and I could tell straight away that Benji had an aura around him. He was a confident guy. It was as if we were old mates.

The first year was a battle for me, trying to get my head around moving to Sydney, being homesick, worrying about whether I had done the right thing. And Benji was still finding his feet a little, seeing which position suited him best.

But by the end of 2004, leading into the 2005 pre-season, everything was starting to come together. We were fit and we were skilful. Tim was big on his skill drills, and Benji's flicks and other tricks were all coming out. They made everyone else feel good. Imagine playing alongside the guy.

'How good's this?' we were thinking. We used to do skill games with five attackers going up against four defenders, having two or three plays to score in a half-field. It was designed to promote ad-lib footy. Benji would just get the ball, step two players and score. We didn't see it all the time, but when he decided to pull a trick out of his bag, we were blown away. After a while, it got to the stage where we just expected it. People watched it at the games and were in awe of it, but we had invariably seen it 20 times before at training.

We were a young squad, and the older guys felt young; they were being rejuvenated by the younger players. Everyone took ownership of the team.

Benji was always confident, off the field as well as on it. I was shocked by what he would say to Tim in team meetings. A few of the boys would giggle, but I just cringed. Some of the stuff he got away with . . . he was borderline rude, but I don't think Tim took offence because it was Benji. I actually think Tim liked it. He'd want to be challenged, and in Benji he had his wish.

The funny thing was, we came out in game one of the 2005 season and got smacked. My brother rang me and said: 'Do you guys do pre-seasons?' Everything we'd done in the off-season turned to dirt. I thought it would be a long year. We were inconsistent during games, and our results followed the same formula. We were very attack-oriented but our defence was questionable. We backed ourselves to score more than we'd concede. It wasn't the ideal way to play, but that's just the type of team we were. Some games, that style would just come off, but others it wouldn't. Benji would try his magic and he'd end up hitting the touch judge.

But when it did come together, we felt like we were at high school. We were just kids having fun, and we got more belief the more we won. It got to the stage where we would take the field and we knew there was no way we were going to get beaten. 'Stick to the plan and we'd bring it home.' I don't know whether there was an arrogance about us, but we were very confident in our ability. Everyone was expecting the bubble to burst, but we just thought: 'What bubble?' All we were doing was winning footy games.

Some we were winning better than others. Just before we played Cronulla in round 21, my daughter was born. It was a hard game, and it was a hot day out at Toyota Park. At halftime, Tim brought me, Benji and Brett Hodgson together. He said: 'When you're jamming that edge, look to shift it wider and cut back under.' Hodgo found himself at dummy half, and Benji wanted the ball out wide. I told him to cut back under me. I went across-field and he dropped late. Then he just went on a rampage, stepping blokes before sending a no-look pass to Daniel Fitzhenry. I went home, grabbed a couple of beers and watched the replay from the couch, as I usually did. I watched that try over and over.

Tim told us all along: 'Don't lock up. Don't die wondering.' We tried not to change too much all year, even down to having the same pairs of shorts and socks for the season. They were ours to wash and bring to the games.

And rather than be intimidated by grand-final week, we embraced it. Hodgo made the point that when he was with Parramatta, playing against Newcastle in 2001, he didn't enjoy the week. Tim Sheens and Royce Simmons shared a few stories about winning and losing grand finals, which hit home to some of us. They both said we'd have some sleepless nights, and they spoke about the opportunity we were presented with. Royce spoke about losing in 1990. He didn't go home for three days. He cried. He doesn't know, to this day, where his runner-up medallion is. It's probably somewhere in the Nepean River, he said.

But when he won it, he didn't come home for a month.

I was that nervous, I pulled the pin on *The Footy Show*. I couldn't eat anything at the grand-final breakfast. But most of the boys just treated it like another game. Look at Benji; he went to a twenty-first the night before, and had Maccas on the way home. I don't think they understood the enormity of it. They were so young and had been so relaxed all year. Why change for the biggest game of your lives? 'We'll worry about losing later.' Nothing really changed. Benji was still dancing and carrying on in the dressing room. I was sitting in my locker thinking I was going to crap myself and he and some of the other boys were dancing.

I still pinch myself about 2005. No one gave us a chance. We'd have days when I'd hit the kid on the grandstand with a pass, Benji would hit a grandmother, and the big boys would curse us for putting them through another scrum. But when it came off . . . Benji was troubled by his shoulders too. I had to make sure I passed at his chest because the strapping meant he couldn't catch the ball up above his head. My job for a lot of that year was just to get him one on one. In that situation, I'd back him against anyone. Make him run.

You always knew when Benji was on. He had a swagger about him. He looked as if he was saying: 'I'll take you to school today.'

I think he'll only get better. At the moment his game is well balanced. That was always going to be the key for him, finding the right balance. He just loves the big-money play and looking good doing it. We all do. But he's mature now; he leads the team, and he takes control of it.

If he falls over, the Tigers are down the tube. That's his value these days.

We had our moments, Benji and me. We'd have defensive meetings with Royce Simmons, then we'd take to the field to practise what he'd told us. I always used to grab Benji and do some extras with him afterwards. It was an opportunity for us to talk, but also to work on our kicking games. We'd kick to each other and play games. Then we'd have lunch together.

One day, after he'd played his first Test, we were kicking the footy together. He said: 'Mate, I've got to go.' 'Why do you have to go?' I said. 'You know we do this all the time.' 'I've got to go to the shops and pay some bills,' he said. I said to him: 'Go then, you don't need to do this because you're a Test star. Just go.' I won't say how he responded. He used to say to me on occasions: 'You're not my dad.' 'I'm not trying to be your dad,' I'd tell him. 'I'm just trying to help you.'

He didn't like me leaving the club. We had always talked about being a partnership. But I was in a difficult position. I went there with a specific mission: play for three years, do my thing, and get out. I had had some serious injuries, and I saw the Tigers as an opportunity to re-establish myself in the NRL. It was a lifeline for me and I was battling my own issues. I had always said that I would be staying for three years and, whatever happened, I'd be returning to Queensland afterwards. It wasn't until I really started to feel a part of something special that I had my doubts. I've thought since about what would have happened if I'd stayed.

I didn't really want to go. I just needed to. It was the hardest decision I've ever had to make. I still imagine being there now, with the team they've got. I love watching them play. Many of them are like family to me, and once you've won a grand final with a group of players, the bond is difficult to break.

There's a photo I still look at. We were back at the leagues club, after the grand final. I was lying on Benji, and he was showing off the ring on his finger. I just remember what we were thinking at the time: 'We've done it.'

Chapter 7

A Label

AND SO, another year, another shoulder surgery. The major difference this time, for my second shoulder reconstruction, at the end of 2005, was that I had company. Dene Halatau needed surgery as well, so I wasn't alone. That made coping with my own a lot easier. Dene went first, and then it was my turn. They shaved my right armpit, drew an arrow on my right arm, and asked me the same questions. 'Right shoulder open reconstruction.' Torturous. I don't remember getting the block the second time; maybe they knocked me out and kept me knocked out. I do remember talking to the anaesthetist, Colin Norgate, who wanted to know all about what it was like to win the comp.

The Tigers doctor, Donald Kuah, wanted to sit in on the operation this time, and I remember waking up on the operating table and saying: 'Nah, that's it, if he's in here, I'm not doing it. I've seen the way he works. I don't trust him.'

I was sharing a room with Dene. After we came out of recovery, his partner brought us back some McDonald's. I'm not sure why, but this time it all stayed down. By this time I lived in an apartment at Westmead. I had my mum with me; she had moved over early in 2005. I knew she and my brothers wanted to move over, but she didn't have the money to do it. I found her a job, through a friend of mine. She and the boys moved into the apartment, I was paying the bills and she was happy. I enrolled the boys at school. It was good to have them there.

I went through pretty much the same recovery as I did following the previous surgery. I had to sleep sitting up. Lots of television. But there was one important difference. I had to learn how to wipe my bottom with my left hand. These are things that you do not think about until they're forced on you. I had a manual car, and would have to change gears while steering with my knees, not being able to use my right hand.

BECAUSE I went under the knife after the season, it was always going to be tight to start the 2006 competition. I rushed a lot of the rehab, because I was so keen to play, and I was so sick of being injured. By the time I returned, in round one against St George Illawarra, I had recovered physically, but mentally I still had a fair way to go. I was whacked in the face in the first half, but I didn't know what I'd done. I carried on, and with about 90 seconds left on the clock, with us down by two points, I set up a try in the corner for winger Michael Crockett. It might just have been one of the freakiest things I've done. I dummied to Paul Whatuira and stepped through Mark Gasnier — their winger came in and without even looking I sent the ball to Michael. We won the game.

It turned out, after scans, that I'd broken my cheekbone. I was told I'd be out for about six weeks, but I was back before then. I returned against the Cowboys, and we were killing them. I'd set up a couple of tries and we looked really good. With about a minute to go, Gavin Cooper ran at me, and I reached out too far with my right arm and, sure enough, pop. It was the second time it had happened in Townsville. It was the second time I'd played there. Gavin heard it go, and he actually apologised. When I later watched the footage, I could see myself trying to yank the joint back into place. I gave it one final effort and it popped back in. I left my arm at my side and tried to walk off casually. I knew the cameras were following me. I just said to the doc, 'Nah.' I stood in the shower under the water for an eternity. I was filthy at the world. Steve Noyce checked on me. He had to help me put my pants on and get my clothes — it was the second time he had to help dress me. I thought everyone was against me. It was so frustrating. I had been so happy to be back and everything just came crashing down on me.

I was confused and angry. I didn't know if it meant the end of me. Channel Nine showed footage of me crying in there, and I was filthy at them for that. I tried to hide away behind the curtains, but the camera just followed me. I didn't want anyone to see me in that state, because I liked everyone to think of me as strong and confident. I didn't want anyone to see me cry, because I couldn't help doing so.

The doctor gave me some painkillers. The team wasn't allowed to drink, but I thought: 'Stuff this, I don't care.' I was so filled with hate. *Stuff it. I don't care any more.* I had a few beers, and I couldn't sleep. I was just lying on the bed in my room. Then it suddenly dawned on me — I hadn't been able to lie down previously. Maybe, I thought, it would be okay this time. I had scans, and while the injury was still a bad one, and the joint would require surgery, there was a silver lining. Previously, the damage was done at the back of the shoulder. This time, though, it was at the front. Very rare, but not as serious as it could have been, I was told. I had the usual options: surgery or rehab. And after what I had got away with in '05, I thought maybe I could be lucky again. I did the rehab again, and I didn't even need a sling it came good so fast.

The Anzac Test in Brisbane was three weeks after that match, and I was desperate to play. I was named in the squad. Tim didn't want me to play, but I'd missed so many Tests already, I just wanted to get out there and be a part of it. I'd had to sit at home while the Kiwis won the Tri-Nations in '05.

Brian McClennan, the Kiwi coach, wanted me to do a fitness test two days out from the game. I had to tackle Steve Matai. To tell the truth I wasn't confident at all, but I just wanted to play. Tim had said he only wanted me to play half a game, because most of my injuries happened under fatigue, when I got lazy. There was even some talk about the insurance premium being too high to allow me to play. I didn't come on until the second half, and by then the game was already out of our reach. Despite the result I was upbeat about my injury. I thought I'd get through the season, as I had the year before, and the Tigers would have another great season.

And for a while it looked like I might be right. I played eight games in a row, and the team was playing well. I played really well against Newcastle and Manly. We were playing against the Panthers in Penrith, and we were down in a close game. I tried a chip and chase, but the Panthers came away with the ball. I scrambled back and tried to dive at one of their players — I think it was Frank Puletua — and I whacked the right joint out of the socket again. I could not believe it.

It was a little different this time, mind you. It was the first time I couldn't let my arm just hang, and I had to hold it up with my left hand. I didn't even bother calling the medical staff. I just walked off, straight up the tunnel. I knew how to manoeuvre myself out of my jumper, having had so much practice. I peeled the jersey off and threw it away. Once again, I got in the shower and didn't want to get out. When I finally did, Royce Simmons was consoling me. I was in shock. I was punching walls with my left hand.

My Uncle Bensy gave me a ride home, and I didn't talk to him. He tried to tell me I'd be okay but I didn't respond. I had lots of telephone messages from my friends; all they wanted to do was reassure me, but I was in such a state that they were really annoying me. I was sick of people feeling sorry for me and I didn't want it. I was in a bad place and I felt very alone.

But, at the same time, I didn't want to be near anyone. I got home and told my mother to leave. I just wanted to be by myself. For three or four days I was like that. I didn't even want to see the doctor, because I knew what was going to happen. I was hearing on the news every day that my career could be over. Every sentence I read about me seemed to begin with the words 'injury prone'— the same old label. Or at least it felt that way.

There were television cameras camped outside Dr Kuah's practice, at Homebush. I knew that sooner or later, I was going to have to see him, but for three days or so I was just in another world. I probably slept for an hour each night. I stared at the TV, and there were times I just sat there and stared at the wall. I ate two-minute noodles here, toast there. I didn't feel hungry. I didn't feel much at all. And for someone who loves having family around, I was in a strange place.

Looking back, I think I needed those three days. Just to cry. I cried morning, afternoon and night. I'd start thinking about the future. *What if I can't play again?* I felt like I was in a dark room, with no windows or doors, no one there to talk to me, and no one to help me. It was like I couldn't hear anything, and I didn't want to hear anything. I was stuck there and I couldn't get out, no matter what I tried.

There were times during those three days that I'd pretty much decided that I was going to just come out and announce my retirement. *I've won a premiership. I've had enough. Is it worth the embarrassment? What if I come back and it happens to me again?* That was scary, because I'd never thought like that, through all my life. If anything happened to me, I'd always just find a way to bounce back and get on top of it. This was the first time I'd really doubted myself.

I turned my phone off for two days. My teammates had been ringing and messaging me. Eventually, I decided to go and see the doc. I was going to need surgery anyway. The cameras were still there when I arrived. I didn't think they'd be there, and I was swamped. I was angry, so with my hood and sunglasses on, and my head down, I barged my way through.

Afterwards, the doc tried to sneak me out the back door. It didn't work; they were still there. They knew where to go.

So I readied myself for surgery again, doing what I had done previously — getting on the drink for a few days to drown my sorrows with a few beers. I didn't go with anyone. It was just me and a schooner glass at the local pub in Westmead. I didn't want to be around anyone.

Not even my family could get hold of me. They were worried about me. There were a lot of things I was saying privately that I probably would never have said before; talking about retirement, not being good enough. They knew where to find me when I checked into the hospital, and many of them came to see me. My teammates, too. Robbie Farah, Dean Halatau, Chris Heighington. From that point on I changed my outlook. I realised how awful it was to be on my own when I had a room full of people around me — Uncle Bensy, all my mates, Steve Noyce, Martin Tauber.

A LABEL

They all come to see me, they all showed support. Steve was unbelievable throughout the whole ordeal. He would ring me every day to see if I was okay and I would always tell him.

He was probably the person I was most honest to about how I was feeling; that I felt like giving away the game.

Sheensy helped, too. He had always made a point of asking me how I was getting on away from footy. When I was injured, he was always calling.

He's always been there for me. He knows what size shorts I wear, he knows where I live, and he probably knows my phone number off by heart. To most people in our team, he is just a coach, but to me he is more than that. We agree to disagree on a lot of things. I could ring him any time of day, about anything, and he would offer advice. He's a father figure to me.

He knew what to say when it came to my injuries. He said he had seen it all before. He told me Mal Meninga broke his arm four times and still went on four Australian tours, and had a great record. 'You can come back from it,' he said. All these things started flicking switches in my mind. I remembered that time when my uncles were picking on me, and I ran home crying, but came back. That fighting instinct came back to me. As soon as I knew I had the support of my family and friends, I felt strong again, or at least stronger. And I wanted everyone around again — I didn't want to be lonely any more. It snapped me out of the mood I was in, and I finally replied to all my messages. I would have had over 150 text messages.

I told the coach I wasn't feeling part of the team. He said: 'Alright, from now on when you train in the morning, you train with the team, and in the afternoon you do what you have to do because you can't train with us.' So I slowly started feeling like I was part of the team again.

Chapter 8

A Final Sling

YOU COULD say I needed a holiday. But the end-of-season trip to Hawaii, in 2006, wasn't exactly what I expected. It started with the group of us who had travelled there — me, Robbie Farah, Jamahl Lolesi, Liam Fulton, Paul Whatuira and Keith Galloway — skinny-dipping in the waters of Waikiki Beach. I'm still not sure how it came to that. Six men nude together on the beach. Now that would have looked strange for anyone looking on (and there were people looking on — some homeless people tried to steal our clothes, which we'd left on the beach).

Then a few days later, at about 4 o'clock one morning, after a night out, we slept through an earthquake. It was a fairly big one. We were on the nineteenth floor of our hotel in Waikiki, and none of us felt it.

It was an experience and a half. The lifts were out, so we had to walk down — and then up — the 19 levels via the stairs. All the power was out in the district. None of the shops or restaurants were open, and I had to line up at one of the corner stores for four hours to buy food, using a torch. I walked out with Spam, Doritos and bread. By the time I got back, Paul had found some food elsewhere and the boys had already eaten.

There was a lot of damage in the area. In our hotel, there

were cracks in the walls and the floors. But we made the best out of a bad situation. You could buy beer in those corner stores so, over the next few days, we were still able to enjoy ourselves. The hotel had a generator so we still had power. It was a great holiday — not what I expected, but still relaxing. It was what I needed.

I HAD a lot of time to prepare for the 2007 season. I was feeling confident again, and I started getting that self-belief to make tackles. I thought: 'Beautiful, I'm back, let's go.' I started talking positively, saying how confident I was to the media. One thing I hated hearing was that I was injury prone. It really struck a nerve. I couldn't wait to prove to the people who were saying it — the media and even the fans — that I wasn't an overpaid crock. A lot of them used to bag me and tell me to give it up. *We don't need him. He's overpaid, he's overrated. Why are we paying him this much money?* I heard the same thing through 2005, then the following year, then the following year . . . I copped it all the time. *Give it up, Marshall.* If someone says I can't do something, it makes me want to do it even more. So 2007 came along and I thought it was a great chance to prove everyone wrong and make amends for all the injuries I'd had.

I'd already been heaped with an extra load. We lost Scott Prince to the Gold Coast Titans, so I had to try to dominate the team a bit more and control the game. I had even more expectation on me from within the team, from the fans, from everyone really. But so far, so good. I was in good form, so much so that people had stopped talking about my injuries.

In round eight, we played Melbourne in Gosford. I'd been training so well and I was that confident, I almost felt back to normal. We started the game well. Then Israel Folau found some space. The only way I could tackle him was to step back on the inside shoulder, my right one, so I jumped up to tackle him and as I was holding on with my right arm, Taniela Tuiaki came in to try to hit Israel from behind, smashing me in the back of the shoulder in the process.

It was by far the most painful out of all of the shoulder injuries. Imagine putting your arm around a pole and then someone driving a truck into the back of your shoulder — your shoulder is thrust forwards and your arm backwards. It felt like I'd snapped my shoulder blade. It was contorted into a position it just wasn't meant for, and it was just so painful. I heard a popping sound again, but it just didn't feel like the other ones. I didn't know what I'd done, although I had a fair idea of what was in front of me. I sat on the sidelines with an ice pack on my shoulder, in my tracksuit, devastated. The TV cameras stalked me — I tried to kick them away on the sideline. I tried to put on a brave face, make it appear like I was calm. On the inside I was hurting so bad.

Afterwards, the team sat down in the dressing room and the coach congratulated them on winning. I was just standing in the corner, and all the boys were looking at me. I remember thinking to myself: 'Don't cry, just don't cry.' The coach said something along the lines of: 'It looks like we're going to lose Benji again for a long part of the season; a lot of you are going to have to stand up.' He said some nice things about me, and then I just started bawling. I had to walk away, but as I did I noticed a few of the boys get a little bit teary, too.

Chris Heighington got up and threw his arm around me. I was an emotional wreck, and I felt like I'd been broken. I couldn't stop crying, and the club had to organise for security to escort me out of the ground. There were still a few fans out the back, and they were trying to get me to sign shirts with my left hand. The last thing I wanted to do was sign autographs, and a couple of people had a go at me. It was the lowest I'd felt. I was just ripped to shreds.

I COULDN'T go to a game for three weeks. Because of the nature of the injury — a fracture in the shoulder socket — I had to have a different sling on. It kept my arm locked at 45 degrees in front of me, and held my arm straight. I had to keep it in that position to make the bone heal properly and in position, and it was very uncomfortable. I couldn't sleep properly.

I had to get away, so I went home to New Zealand. I told the coach, 'I've got to go home,' and he told me to take whatever time I needed.

My family were devastated for me. I sat with Mick and Annalie and we were all crying. They put their arms around me, we had a big hug, and I thought to myself: 'Maybe I should just come back here and stay. I'm feeling good here. No one can get me, no one can doubt me, no one can judge me.'

I was so close to staying. I was ready to just pack it in. *Now is probably a good time to forget about it, just be happy with where you've got to, just give it away.* There was a little sunroom at the house, where the family used to just sit and talk. I spent a lot of time sitting in there during the day, watching the sun shining through the windows. Mum would always be in the kitchen, doing her own thing but also watching me. She knew something was very wrong.

I didn't want anyone around me except my mum and dad. Mick would go and work on the tractors; sometimes I'd go for a ride with him in his truck and just sit down and talk about things.

After a week, I was meant to return to Sydney, but I said to Annalie: 'Mum, I don't want to go back yet.' I changed my flight.

I went for a ride with Dad in the truck and I said to him: 'I'm thinking maybe that's it for me, maybe I should just finish up and let it go.' I told him I was finding it hard to deal with. He was probably the only person I could have said that to. He was the only person I didn't feel embarrassed to be saying it to. Because my uncles are so tough, I felt embarrassed to be saying that I was struggling to do something to them. I always wanted to prove to them that I could do something, but when it looked like I might not be able to, it was Mick I spoke to.

We were in the paddock, checking on the cows, and he stopped the truck and looked at me. 'You know what matters the most?' he asked me. 'All that matters are the people that matter to you. Who matters to you?' he added. 'Family,' I replied. 'Well, all that matters is what your family says. Who else matters?' 'My friends,' I replied. 'The only people who can judge you are the people who know you,' he said. He never, ever, swore, but he said, 'Stuff what the media says, stuff what everyone else says. It doesn't matter. We're your family and I'm telling you you're good enough to come back. There are a lot of things you can still do in the game. You do a lot of work on your body, get it physically up to it, and you'll be alright.' I think Mum wanted me to stay home, didn't want me to go back, but Dad always pushed me in the right direction, always made me think about my decisions before I made them. When I was thinking about signing with rugby union, I was very keen, but he didn't think it was the right move. 'You should stay with rugby league,' he said. He would always end up being right.

In this case, he said: 'Go back to training, see how it feels, get around your teammates and friends, get the feeling back, and if you don't enjoy the training and you don't want to be there, you can always come home.'

By this stage, I could feel a little more movement in my shoulder. I started playing tennis left-handed. I'd hold the ball in my left hand, chuck it up, grab the racquet and serve. It made me think that if I can pick up left-handed tennis that fast, surely I could get back to what I'm already good at. If I tried to play left-handed tennis now I couldn't, but back then it made me understand that if I could learn a new skill like that and improve, surely I could relearn an old one.

I started training hard, real hard, as hard as you could possibly imagine. There was a fire deep inside me, driving me to train harder and get fitter than I'd ever been. I'd put on a bit of weight from going home and being on the drink for a while and eating junk, so I had to work it off. I enjoyed it.

I came back and played before the end of the season. I had surgery at the end of it. The surgeon took bone from my hip and grafted it to my shoulder. He took photographs and showed them to me afterwards, telling me I had mild arthritis, which was going to get worse. It is as if I have 50-year-old shoulder joints in a 26-year-old body. Much of the time, nowadays, I just feel grinding in the right joint. I will probably need a shoulder replacement before I am 40. I'm not too worried about that at the moment; it's all about the now for me. I'll worry about getting a new shoulder when I need to. I'm going to get old, and I know my body is just going to fail one day. Something has to give when you have had so many operations. But as long as I'm alright now, when I'm playing, I don't care.

On cold mornings, it takes me a good hour to warm my shoulder up. Getting out of bed can sometimes be difficult. I have to get out on my left side. I can feel a deep ache. I will have to take a glucosamine tablet every day for the rest of my life for the arthritis. I hate taking tablets; I try not to take Panadol when I'm sick. I am a big believer in the body's natural healing powers. I hated doing weights until I realised that I needed to. I'm stubborn like that, just like my mum. But that stubbornness has helped, too. After that last shoulder surgery, I was determined to come back better. I didn't even give myself a break over Christmas.

Much of this information, I have had to check. Many of my injuries blend into each other. And I have found that the best way to try to get over them is to attempt to forget them. I have to try to convince myself that they have not happened. I read about a study from a US university which showed that, in repeat injuries, the biggest battle is in the mind. It's never the actual injury which prevents you from playing again. It's always the mind. I can understand that.

Whenever things were tough, I was always very good at convincing myself that nothing was wrong. I don't know how I got through it.

I do consider myself mentally tough. Occasionally, it all builds up and gets the better of me. Everyone has a breaking point. I think the trigger for me was the fact that I had convinced myself so many times that I was going to be okay, so when I kept getting injured it was difficult to believe. I had continual disappointment. That's when I was at my lowest, when I thought about giving in.

IN 2008, there was so much scrutiny on me. It resurrected a lot of stuff that I didn't want to see and hear any more, highlights of me dislocating my shoulder — not just the last one, but the previous three. It brought back a lot of hate.

I knew it shouldn't be a motivator, but I wanted to shut up the people who were doubting me. The Tigers extended my contract by one year, giving me the chance to prove myself. I'd never been more amped about a season.

And so, of course, three minutes into my comeback, in round one against the Dragons at the Sydney Football Stadium, I was tackled by Matt Cooper, stood up and couldn't feel my knee. I could not believe it. It was hurting. But having never suffered a knee injury, I didn't know how serious it was, or what it was. I thought at first that I'd torn my anterior cruciate ligament, and that was it. Career over. The doctor came on to assess me, but he couldn't tell what I'd done. He told me to come off the field. I tried to walk off as freely as I could, without limping. It was hurting like hell, but I tried to be brave.

The doctor told me that rather than damaging my ACL, I had torn my PCL, the posterior cruciate ligament. I said: 'What's that mean?' He said: 'It depends.' So I was back for another MRI, the only saving grace being that because it was my knee, only my leg was in there. At least I could keep my eyes open.

The doctor told me I'd suffered a ruptured PCL. He showed me the model of a knee, and said it was like taking the ligament that holds the outside of your knee together and ripping it in half. It was so uncomfortable. I said: 'Do I need surgery?' He told me some people have surgery to repair it, and some just play on without it. I played on, always thinking that if something else happened, it would be the end of me. 'At least it's not my shoulder' was the line I was giving the media.

Four weeks later, I returned against the Knights in Newcastle. I could run, but with a limp. I put up a bomb and it just landed straight back in my hands, while I basically limped over the line for a try. Robbie Farah threw me the ball, I put a right-foot step on Chris Houston, and I had Wes Naiqama to beat. I ran around him, and on one leg, limped to the tryline. The commentators couldn't believe how bad I was limping, but I still scored the try.

It was the hardest game I had had to play in terms of physical pain, but I just made sure I got through it. We won, but I had to miss the next match — my knee was playing up again. I came back the week after to play Cronulla, and with my first run of the ball, I stepped someone and felt it click. I panicked. 'I've done it again.' At halftime, I told the doctor, and he needled me up. I didn't realise it, but that's what happens with the PCL — sometimes it just clicks.

I got through the game, and ended up having a decent run. But I do feel that if I had suffered another injury that year, it would have been the end of me. Emotionally, I don't think I would have been able to handle it. Now, if I get injured again, I feel I would have the ability, and the mental capacity, to come back from it. Back then, though, it was just such an emotional time. Physically, of course, it was regularly difficult. I wasn't able to bench press from 2004 until 2010, because of my shoulders. They just didn't have the range of movement to carry it out. I could stretch my arms out, but bringing them back to my chest was just about impossible. My shoulders would feel like they were just about to break. I couldn't do chin-ups either. Thus, it was difficult to build up my strength when I couldn't do those exercises. I still use a block when I bench press, to stop the bar dropping too far.

My shoulder injuries affected me in defence, too. I was never a bad defender when I was younger. But when your confidence goes, the ability to tackle goes with it. I was constantly trying to protect my shoulders, which felt like the right thing to do, but that was affecting the way I tackled.

I'll be the first to admit that I was a poor tackler throughout those years. I missed a lot of tackles, ones that I should have made. It took a lot of work to get that confidence back. I had to change my tackling, get up quicker. The problem I had was that I used to let the attacking players run to me. Now I go to them. I cut down their time as well as the force they take into the tackle.

I got the big guys to run at me to bring the confidence back. Darren Senter helped me out a lot, as did Mark O'Neill. Chris Heighington was probably the biggest influence. He made me do it, which I needed on the odd occasion, because there were times I was scared of what might happen to my shoulders. I'm not afraid to admit that I was scared. I was scared of losing my career. It was hard for me to actually want to tackle somebody. 'Just 12 today,' Chris would say, or 'just six'. I'd do it. For two years, 2007–08, Chris grabbed me after just about every training session — and saved me.

There were suggestions for a while that I would be moved to fullback as a result of my injuries. But I liked defending in the front line. Tim tossed it up a number of times. He gave me a long speech in his office about why he wanted to do it. I gave him a very short answer. 'No.' I know he was only looking out for me, because of my shoulders. But why do it? I did so much organising. I always felt that would be so much harder from the back. In defence, too, I would have felt more isolated at fullback. If the opposition made a break, I would be on my own. When you defend in the front line at least you have some support. To be honest, I think Tim was testing me, to see how keen I was to make tackles in the front line.

For a long time, I was considered a liability. And it hurt. But it just made me want to improve, and prove to anyone who saw me that way that I was far from a liability. No one likes to see

A FINAL SLING

those things written about them. You can say: 'It doesn't affect me.' But I don't think that's possible. In the environment we, as football players, are in we are all competitive and proud. When someone questions whether you are good enough, whether you are tough enough, are you seriously going to believe that it has no impact on you? Of course it will dent your ego. I knew why they were saying I was a liability. Maybe it was fair. But I still didn't like to hear it.

I probably didn't lose the little voice in the back of my head, the one saying, 'Don't put your shoulders in that position,' until 2008.

The hardest thing about a long-term injury, though, is not feeling part of a team. When they were training outside, I was inside. When they were doing contact work, all I could do was watch. I felt like I was excluded, pushed away; knowing that I would go to every game but couldn't help.

What got me through was having guys like Dene Halatau, Robbie Farah and Chris Heighington saying to me: 'Bagz, we'll do this as a team.' I never, ever felt like I was in the team when I was injured. It was a dark place. Dene would ring me every day, and the chief executive at the time, Steve Noyce, would ring me every week. Tim would ring me, my Uncle Bensy would ring me, my mum and dad, my brothers, doctors, physios.

Tim would ring me and give me advice removed from football. There were a couple of occasions Tim told me to have surgery, have the season off and come back the following season. 'As a coach, I should tell you to strengthen it for six weeks. As a friend I'm telling you not to.' I'd reply: 'I appreciate that. Too bad, I'm playing.'

I realise now that I should have listened to him and others on occasions. I should have been smarter. I was always too keen to return. You'd think I would have learnt after four reconstructions. It was just my nature. I wanted to help the team and not let anyone down. I'd rather play at 70 percent than not play at all. I don't regret anything, though. Maybe '05 wouldn't have happened.

Without my friends and family, there's a good chance I could have given the game away. There were stages when I thought: 'This is it for me.' I didn't know if I wanted to play any more. I didn't know if I was good enough to play any more. Those were things I never thought I'd be thinking, but it was hard not to. Ever since I was a kid, I wanted to be, well, awesome. But was it worth the embarrassment? The papers were saying I was injury prone, and that my career was going to be over before I knew it. Deep inside, I knew it could be.

Tim Sheens

WHEN I think of Benji fighting back from all his injuries, I think of Mal Meninga. I also think of Joe Vitanza. Joe played under me at Penrith; a big, strong kid. His knee collapsed in a tackle. He was the player who ultimately changed a rule; after he was hurt, players were allowed to hand the ball to someone else to play the ball if the tackled player was injured, rather than being forced to play the ball or lose possession. Joe got up and played the ball, while the bottom part of his leg was just dangling there. He'd torn every ligament. His leg was just swinging below the knee. Bryan Hyder, our trainer, was holding onto him as he rolled the ball between his legs. Then he was carried off.

The surgeons tightened Joe's knee so much that he had a stiff leg. He couldn't bend it for a long time. Then he had to work hard just to run. It was almost two years before he played again, but he did. He played in the 1990 grand final as a replacement. Mal came back after four broken arms.

A FINAL SLING

Benji knew little about either of them, but I told him if he persevered, he could come back.

I'm not sure what it was about him. Some players just have a propensity for injuries. Some joints just aren't as strong as others. He wasn't very heavy-set through the shoulders. His background was touch football, too, so he didn't play a lot of contact football as a kid. He didn't have the standard background of junior representative sides, where they get beaten up a little. He was a skinny little thing early on, a fine player but with a fine build.

When I'd talk with Benji about his shoulder problems, I'd use Mal Meninga as the example. Repeat injuries, whether they're shoulders, knees or anything, really depress players. They shatter them. Mal wore the big arm guard for years, and wasn't real keen to throw his arm into the tackle. Benji was very tentative for a while. To this day, he is attacked by the big runners. But he's a lot bigger and stronger now, and he can put a lot more body in the tackles.

I don't think he's been given enough credit for his comebacks. No one could really understand unless they've been through the psychological problems and the long periods of rehab, the constant wondering whether your career is over before it started. He had that worry; Benji was worried his career was over. He was never afraid of being injured, but he was worried about losing his career before he even got started. He was young and he had plenty in front of him. We knew what a good player he was going to be and so did he. But those sorts of injuries have finished some players. You just have to keep working with them, give them your experience, tell them if you persevere you'll get through it. We made sure everyone stayed close to him, and he stayed close to us. We gave him things to do; he'd watch our games, trying to learn more.

He'd come to the team meetings. When players are on the injured list, they don't feel part of the team any more. You've got to work hard to keep them close to the boys and make them feel useful, make them feel wanted. You've got to keep them interested, keep them busy, and somehow try to get the time to pass by as quickly as you can. Injured players spend a lot of time in rehab and it's a terrible place to be, especially with your arm in a sling.

Anyone who thinks footballers are overpaid should listen to coaches when they tell players: 'You must risk injury playing. You can't play soft; you have to run hard and tackle hard otherwise you don't survive.' These players are risking injury every time they go into a tackle or run the ball. I have a huge appreciation for what they do. I often tell players: 'You are going to spend time in hospital.' I tell them before they start their careers. I tell the young blokes to get used to the fact they are going to visit the specialist at some stage.

The blokes who play this sport are the first ones out of the trenches in war. They are the alpha males, the big, athletic kids at school, not afraid of anything. If you're not that way, you play other sports. Benji played this sport and he's one of the toughest I've seen in the toughest of sports.

My first recollection of Benji was when Steve Lavers, who had forged the link with Keebra Park, was telling me about him. I played him in the Colts game against the Roosters at Campbelltown and I knew then that we had a good kid.

When I gave him his NRL debut, I really had no choice. At the time we were on a $3 million cap, even though the NRL salary cap was $600,000 higher. The joint venture was in financial trouble. Neither Wests nor Balmain would guarantee the club any more than $3 million. If we spent over that we were in trouble. Part of that cap was also paying for those young kids, the likes of Robbie Farah, Bryce Gibbs, Liam Fulton and Benji.

So he came into first grade in tough times. He was always confident. The first autograph he signed was a mile long and was finished with a crown on top. He signed it in the gym and the other boys just jumped on him over it. They quickly pulled him into line. He was super cocky.

We used to train down at Lidcombe Oval in the weeks before

A FINAL SLING

Christmas. The team was doing a training run, up and down the field. My assistant coach, Royce Simmons, said to him: 'Have a go, son.' So Benji ran past everyone, leapt over a big pile of tackle bags, which was in the middle of the oval, waved at Royce and kept going. It was a fair pile of tackle bags, but he just upped his stride and jumped over it as if it wasn't there. Royce said: 'I'd kill that kid — if I could catch him.' He was a true athlete, super quick, clever, and confident in himself from the beginning. He could be a wild kid; we had to pull him into line a few times. But I always say there is no use putting an old head on a 19-year-old. He's got to go through the 19-year-old thing. He had a stud in his ear worth more than I earned.

The thing about him was he always trained. When you take away the serious injuries, I can count on my hands the number of training sessions he has missed. He can be sick and he'll train. And he can lift a training session with his attitude. He's always been great in that area, which I use as one marker for players. If they've got talent and are great trainers, the chances are you've got yourself a pretty good player. That is Benji.

The great players who didn't train . . . you look back on them and you say they could have been anything. They could have been greater if they trained. But this kid, from day one, never missed a beat.

That's why I didn't mind the flick passes (dare I say I used one occasionally here and there myself). He practised them at training and also on the touch football field, which I could never get him off.

The grand-final one, though? That was out of the box. The confidence to do it on first tackle was something else. I put it up there with the memorable ones from the 1989 grand final, John 'Chicka' Ferguson's try or Steve Jackson's. Every grand final has one, or in that case of 1989, two. Some are more memorable than others. I didn't actually see Benji's flick at the time. Before I realised anything had happened, Patty Richards had the ball and I was cheering him home. On replay, like everyone else, I saw what had happened. I wasn't overly shocked, though. He always had that ability. He always reminded me of Steve Mortimer and Anthony Mundine. He has Mundine's feet, and the chip and chase. I was watching footage recently of Bob Fulton, and I told 'Bozo' that he reminded me of Benji. They were all great running players with footwork and ability. Even at Benji's age, Bob Fulton made other players look like they were standing in cement. He moved past people that quick — and he was cheeky about it, too. Mortimer had unpredictability, great speed and anticipation.

I'll wonder sometimes what Benji is doing. Sometimes he looks like he doesn't know what he's doing. But he does. He's probing. Mundine did the same, as did Mortimer. They'll duck out of a hole and into the next hole, then beat you with pace. They're free-running players.

Most people will often think those types of player don't play to a game plan; they'll just zigzag and end up wherever they get to. That doesn't mean they don't know the game. Benji knows the game as well as anyone I've coached. Some people have to play it to see it, while with others you have to draw it on a board for them. Others still can see it in their minds as you talk about it. They generally sit up the front of the meeting room. That's Benji. The smarter ones sit up the front, like they would at school. They can visualise what you are saying. Most of the really good players see it as you see it.

With his background in league, or lack of it originally, and his shoulder problems, I have no doubt Benji is yet to play his best football. When I say his best football, I mean a more structured game. He tends to play what he sees and sometimes that goes against what we're trying to do. He didn't play a lot of football before he was a first-grader, and he's had a lot of time out. His whole rugby league education has been in the past eight years or so. He is not that prototype player who has been playing since he was seven and has been through S.G. Ball and Harold Matthews, and had the coaching all the way.

He has picked it up incredibly quickly, considering. Our fortunes have often fluctuated on his shoulders. That's the ability he has. We didn't have

A FINAL SLING

the depth or the money to have another five-eighth or another halfback ready to go if we lost him. I believe that, over the next few years, we will see his best footy; seeing the game better. He's finding a calmness and a confidence which both come with playing more football. Hopefully, he will be injury-free. Even if he loses some of his speed, he will still be quick. And he's 90-metre quick, too — not too many halfbacks possess that. He has fullback speed, wing speed.

I often thought that he could actually play fullback. I told him once not to worry about his shoulders because if it came to it, I could just turn him into the world's best fullback, out of a busy defensive line but still in the game.

Darren Lockyer was still a great fullback; Matt Bowen was a very good five-eighth, just not physically big enough for the front line. Fullbacks used to be kick-returners, not ball-players; Garry Jack, Gary Belcher. Darren pioneered the ball-playing fullback, the No. 1 who can play like a second or third five-eighth. Benji could do it if it came to that.

One on one is when he is the most dangerous; in less traffic, with a bit more space, he is very hard to handle. In that try in the grand final, people forget he was returning the ball as a winger, from the corner. The flick was the end of it, but he'd beaten three and off he went. Greg Alexander, Phil Blake . . . they're all similar in that they had fullback traits in the halves.

Benji can run the length of the field to score and his support play is something he is not given a lot of credit for. It's the same with his cover defence. Greg Alexander used to stop countless tries and Benji is the same. If someone makes a break, Benji will pick someone off to help the fullback make a decision.

As a coach, I'm looking at those little one-percenters, the extra efforts players make in a game. Even if they aren't able to stop something, they're trying to. Not too many react like Benji does. As soon as there is any sort of line break, he's gone. Darren is the same in that regard.

I am not suggesting Benji would be a better fullback, mind you.

BENJI

I am saying that he could play any role in the backline. I played him in a trial as a centre and he scored. He just beat people; get him the ball and get him running. The reason he played five-eighth so quickly is he wanted to. He wanted to get his hands on the ball. I've never been able to get it off him.

Chapter 9

God Defend Me

I NEVER realised how much I wanted to represent New Zealand until I played against the Kiwis. Until I faced the haka. The first time I did so came when I played for Australia, at the touch football World Cup in Japan.

Every kid in New Zealand is taught to do the haka. I can guarantee that just about everyone in New Zealand knows the actions and the words because just about everyone in New Zealand is an All Blacks supporter. New students are welcomed to a school with a haka. I was taught it as far back as I can remember, and I always dreamed of participating in one for New Zealand. I never imagined I'd be facing one on a football field.

I played for Australia more out of revenge than anything else. I didn't feel like I was getting a fair go in New Zealand; I played for the Bay of Plenty in the national championships, in Rotorua in March 2000. I was player of the tournament. But I still didn't make the New Zealand men's team. Then when I moved to Australia, I missed out again. Out of sight, out of mind, I guess.

One of my best mates, Tony Trad, who is still the coach of the Australian men's touch team, picked me and my best mate, Drummayne Dayberg, in the mixed team. Drummy, who is probably the best touch player in the world at the moment, and

I were both Kiwis, but we were both filthy at the New Zealand selectors for not picking us.

New Zealand's mixed side was just about the pinnacle of touch football; they had dominated the world for about a decade. The side included Pete Walters, who was a legendary touch player, the master of inventive football. He is considered the best player ever to play touch. If we couldn't play with him we'd have to play against him. So we travelled to Japan for the World Cup, mid-2003, and had the time of our lives. I met some of the best people I've ever come across. It was the first time I'd ever been anywhere other than New Zealand or Australia. The tournament was in Kumagaya, about an hour out of Tokyo. The trip was a big culture shock for me; I didn't like the food much so I ate mostly McDonald's. I had it every night, I'd say, just having to point at the burger and give finger signals. *Three of that burger, two of that one, chips, drink.* I knew how to count in Japanese, and then the odd word on top of that, but not knowing any more of the language made life there difficult.

The scenery was beautiful, and so were the karaoke bars. I was a bit of a rebel in those days, so the night before the World Cup started I was at one particular bar with the coach and a few of the other players, sinking schooners and singing off-key. We only had to play Thailand in the morning, we thought. We did beat them comfortably.

Some of the people I got to know in Japan are still some of my best mates. Those friendships helped me survive in Sydney; when I played in the tournament I was still living on the Gold Coast, but when I moved to Sydney I at least knew some people who I had been with on that tour. Jamie Stowe got me drunk on scotch for the first time in Japan, and some of my teammates found me in the gutter. He became one of my best mates and took me under his wing when I moved to Sydney.

We made the final and, sure enough, faced New Zealand. Which meant I came face to face with the haka. I actually felt like doing one in response; Drummayne and I advanced on the Kiwis and we got into a push and shove with some of the Kiwi players. At the time I was young, immature and just wanted revenge for not being picked. Obviously, living in Australia, it was hard for the selectors to see us play, but we always felt like we were good enough to represent New Zealand. We won the competition, and I was player of the tournament, so I guess we were right.

WHEN I returned from Japan, I headed straight for Kingaroy, where I represented the South Coast in a Queensland Schoolboys trial, playing against Karmichael Hunt. I played the very same day I returned to the country. From there, I made the Queensland Schoolboys squad.

I knew about the culture of playing for Queensland at State of Origin level, but I didn't really think too hard about it when I played for the Maroons at schoolboy level. It was just a means to have a good time. But some started to talk about the prospect of me playing for Queensland.

The Junior Kiwis squad was named before the Australian Schoolboys team was selected. I missed out on that squad, so the coach of the Australian team, Rod Pattison, said he'd have me in his team. By then I'd already played first grade for the Tigers, but I didn't hesitate in playing. Revenge was at the forefront of my mind again, especially as the tour took in Wellington, Palmerston North and Auckland, places I loved. I played alongside Sam Perrett, a Kiwi now but an Aussie Schoolboy like me back then, Karmichael, Heath L'Estrange, Brett Anderson and Tom Learoyd-Lahrs. We won two and lost one. That tour, more than anything else, made me realise I wanted to play for New Zealand. Standing there, watching the team I wanted to be in do the haka to me, was awful. I was miming the words while they did it. I sang the New Zealand national anthem under my breath. 'What am I doing here?' I thought. 'I shouldn't be here. This is wrong.' My family, proud New Zealanders, were in the crowd supporting Australia. Because of me.

The Kiwis obviously had a plan to get into me, because on the first tackle, the fullback ran straight at me. I spear-tackled him and an all-in brawl followed; Louis Anderson running in and throwing punches, Manu Vatuvei and Iosia Soliola ripping in. 'You traitor,' they'd say to me. I did feel bad, and I really didn't want to play after that first game. It was difficult to get motivated when I wanted to be on the other side. I wanted to be a Kiwi.

So by the time I was asked which country I wanted to represent, I was able to answer straight away. I knew it would break my family's heart if I chose to play for Australia. It was different at schoolboy level. If I was playing for Australia now, I truly believe my family would be devastated. They'd be cheering for me, but deep down . . . well I know what I'd be thinking, anyway.

There was an enormous amount of pressure on me at the time I made my decision. Sure, I'd played first grade, but I was still a schoolboy. 'Is he a Kiwi or a Kangaroo?' I knew I wanted to play for New Zealand, but not knowing how to handle the media, who wanted to know yesterday, I was confused. I painted what I was feeling on a canvas in art class at Keebra Park. I called the work 'Taonga'.

This is what I wrote at the time to describe it:

This work sets out to portray the difficulty of making a decision between playing for Australia or New Zealand. It was definitely a personal reflection on all the media pressure upon me and by explaining it on canvas I was able to relieve some stress. The pressure was phenomenal.

The photo selected features the tattoo, which is a cultural symbol. The colours black/white and green/gold symbolise the dilemma the media focus imposed on me. The tribal symbols represent my family and what is most important to me. The use of text creates a focal point. 'Taonga' means sacred and special or treasured. My intention with the use of mixed media and spontaneous paint application was to emphasise confusion and the difficulty of the decision-making process. This piece may have become a bit 'overworked' in parts but I believe the message was clear and I found it a useful expressive exercise. — Benji Marshall

I was so young back then. I felt like I didn't have time to make a proper choice. Few people in New Zealand knew who I was. They might have after my NRL debut, but clearly not before it. I look back now and think that I was never going to choose Australia over New Zealand, but it was still a difficult, and rushed, decision for me. The painting portrayed how I was feeling. The decision was a sacred one. It wasn't about representing myself; it was about representing my family and my country.

That's not to say I regret playing touch or Schoolboys for

Australia. But I certainly do not regret my decision to squander any chance of playing State of Origin by choosing to play for the Kiwis. I was born in New Zealand, so I'm a Kiwi. That's how it should be. Karmichael went a different way. He wanted to play State of Origin. Good luck to him. But that was his decision, and everyone is entitled to make their own choice. I'm sure there were a lot of people filthy at me for choosing to play for Australia at touch and schoolboy level — and beating New Zealand into the bargain. Hopefully, I've righted some of those wrongs while wearing the black jumper later on.

I DIDN'T have to wait too long to start. My name was tossed up in 2004, but I was injured shortly before the team for the Anzac Test of that year was selected. I couldn't tour at the end of that year either, having to undergo shoulder surgery. But in 2005, even though I was injured in the first club trial, I made my first New Zealand squad. Daniel Anderson, who was the coach, telephoned me and said: 'Congratulations, you made the team.'

I was only 20, and I had been given something that I dreamed of as a kid. I'd always wanted to represent my country and I had always wanted to do the haka, and sing the New Zealand anthem, in front of a big crowd. I phoned Uncle Phil first, then Uncle Bensy. Phil was emotional and Bensy was in tears. I tried to get around to just about everyone in my family; my grandfather was over the moon. In a way, it meant more to my family than it did to me. Don't get me wrong, I was happy to be there. But at the same time, I was probably happier to be able to represent my family. I used to be the spoilt little smart-arse back in those days, so to be able to stand there in the first team photo . . . it meant a lot to me to be the source of pride and joy for the family.

I was quieter than normal that week. I'd played 19 games for the Tigers, and I was playing against Darren Lockyer for my country, wearing the same number as he was. I was playing with men like Ruben Wiki, Nathan Cayless and Nigel Vagana, with Nigel being my roommate. They were all legends of the game, and they were my teammates. That didn't really faze me because I was so young, confident, keen and a little cocky. I didn't feel like a player who had notched up fewer than 20 games.

I had played those games over three seasons, due to all of my injuries, and I had learnt a lot about the game just watching it. When I was injured, I studied the game from the bench or the coach's box. I listened closely to what Tim Sheens told the team. I actually think I learnt a lot more by watching than I did by playing. When it came to playing the Test, I felt like I'd been playing for three full seasons.

And I was happy to be there. It was like being back in New Zealand, and we were like a family. I quickly went from calling people mate to bro and cuz again. You always get your New Zealand accent back when you go into camp.

IT WAS an away Test match for us, but it felt like home to me. We were in camp on the Gold Coast, at the Crown Plaza, not far from the casino. On the first night, we went to the casino, and then played poker in the team room until about 3 a.m. I lost most of my allowance for the trip to David Kidwell. He was called 'The Eraser' because he used to take everyone out. I was just so stoked to be around those guys, so I didn't really care that I'd lost my money. They were talking to me. I was in the crew. As long as I was there playing, nothing else mattered.

We moved to Brisbane the night before the game. When I

arrived in the foyer of the hotel, about to get on the team bus out to Suncorp Stadium for the Test, I saw two police motorbikes. I thought: 'What have the boys done here?' I was so young and naive, I didn't realise they were part of our police escort. It freaked me out a bit. The Prime Minister gets a police escort. I don't get a police escort.

Down Caxton Street, I was certainly glad they were there. When all the fans saw the New Zealand team bus on the famous pub strip, they started banging it. I had my headphones on, the volume up and my head down.

Steve Noyce had flown some of my relatives to Brisbane, including my mum, my brothers and Uncle Bensy, for that Anzac Test. I knew where they were sitting — halfway up the grandstand, in a box. So as I was singing the anthem, I looked up to try to see them. One of my brothers was waving a flag, while my mum was in tears. So was I — trying to hold them in because the TV camera was moving past me. I looked down. We huddled up before we did the haka.

When I do the haka now, I try to concentrate on one player in the opposition. Back then I used to look at all of them, trying to see who was freaking out and who wasn't. I was so psyched, I honestly felt like I could have killed someone.

We lost that game, but I was still satisfied and just happy to be there. I set up a try; chipped and regathered on the last tackle, stepping past someone with my right foot before sending a no-look pass to Frank Pritchard. He drew and passed to Matt Utai. All in all, I had a fairly solid debut. It was my first Test and the try I helped set up is what I remember most, not the feeling of losing it. If I lose nowadays I am filthy, no matter how I play. But back then I was young and a little indifferent. I was happy to be among those players.

BRIAN MCCLENNAN took over as coach midway through 2005 and led the side into the Tri-Nations tournament of later that year, in England. I was devastated to miss it, having to watch them win from home, still recovering from shoulder surgery following the NRL season. I was happy for them, sure, but disappointed I couldn't be there.

It was difficult to watch, I guess a bit like watching your team win the premiership when you're not out there. I was hurt again early in '06, but I was named to play for the Kiwis even though I had yet to return for the Tigers after being injured.

My Tigers coach, Tim Sheens, said he'd only allow me to be picked if I played half a game. His reasoning was that my shoulders used to pop when I was fatigued and making poor decisions in defence. That and I hadn't played for more than a month. I didn't want to start off the bench, but Tim had put his five cents in and I had to cop it. By the time I came on, the game was already lost.

I did get to play with Sonny Bill Williams, the only half of football I have been able to do so. Over the years, either I was out or he was. That was our only opportunity to play together. That was frustrating.

I would have loved to have played a lot more with him. We could have done some real damage. Imagine the results if he'd been playing with us every Test since that night. We could have been *really* dominant. I got 40 minutes to build up a combination with him. It's a regret that I wasn't able to play more with him. Who knows? He might come back.

THINGS WERE clearly changing for us, despite that result. The belief Brian McClennan was instilling was incredible. I understood how he had managed to take the team to the Tri-Nations title.

He had a way of bringing the boys together. The Mad Butcher, Peter Leitch, was an important part of that change, too, as the team manager that year. He is one of the greatest men I've ever met in my life. He never wants or expects any recognition for the charity work he does, providing everything from meat to money for the children's hospital in Auckland. If my family needed tickets for the game, he'd get them for me. He still phones me every couple of weeks to see how I'm going. If something happens to me, he is always making sure I'm okay. He has always been there for the players.

The Butcher introduced a tradition: when a player came into the squad, he was given a pendant of a greenstone koru (a spiral like an uncurling fern frond). It was the Butcher's way of making sure all the boys stayed connected, wherever they were in the world. We were a family, and we all had one of these pendants, attached to a black neckband.

Now, we have dog tags as well, with our name and playing number engraved on them. I'm player number 717. If anyone is caught without their koru or their dog tags at certain times during camps, they could be fined, made to sing a song or perform a haka on their own.

Really, I shouldn't have played that half a game in 2006. I was underdone. I wasn't ready, not for club football, so certainly not for a Test. But I was happy I did play. I missed too many Test matches over the years through injury, so even playing one, or a half of one, when I probably shouldn't have was still worth it. I would not get to pull on the black jersey again until 2008. In between, I was a commentator for one of the Tests, an emcee during a Tigers function for another. It was hardly the same.

Bensy Marshall

BENJI COULD have played for Australia. Not just because he played his early rugby league in the country, but because he is actually part-Australian. Just a small part of him, but a part of him nonetheless. Benji's great-great-grandfather was born in Tasmania. He also has a bit of Scottish ancestry, which most would not know about the New Zealand captain.

I saw him face the haka, wearing the Australian colours. I took my dad, his grandfather, to see him. We were cheering for Australia, but we did feel strange. To see him representing New Zealand later . . . words can't describe how we felt and how we feel. Every time the team sings the national anthem or does the haka, the hairs stand up on the back of my neck. My brothers feel exactly the same.

It feels extra special for me. I was christened Benjamin. My mum had a strong Maori accent, and couldn't say Benji. I just became Bensy.

I walked into the hospital when my sister Lydia had given birth and said: 'Benjamin's a good name.' I was just joking, really. But the next day, she told us: 'I've named him Benjamin.' I was so proud. I was married about three or four years later, to Michelle, Mick and Annalie's daughter. Benji was our page boy. I always had a soft spot for him. I'd pick him up at weekends and take him to Mick and Annalie's. Every time he runs out, whether it be for the Tigers or New Zealand, I just want to stand up and say: 'I know that dude.'

Lydia used to leave him with her friends on occasion and I'd round him up. 'I'm here to pick up Benjamin.' 'Who are you?' 'Don't worry about who I am? I'm here to pick him up.' Michelle and I used to love him like he was our own. I used to work at a dairy factory. I remember taking Benji to Christmas parties there, and when I was asked, 'Is this your son?' I'd reply, 'Yeah.'

I always wanted Benji to have what I, and the rest of my brothers, did not. Most of my brothers left home when they were young. Our home used to burst at the seams. We would have bread and what we called 'boil-up' for dinner. It was basically meat, cabbage and potatoes, piled in a big pot and boiled up. It's what we used to live on. I was given plum jam on bread every day — to this day, I can't stand plum jam. We were rationed, and we had to be. I slept with three other brothers in a double bed. David used to hand his clothes down to Luke, Luke to Bussy, and Bussy to me. We didn't know any different. I was given a new pair of shoes when Mum was given a good benefit, maybe every 18 months or so.

Every street had its big families and Kiwi Street had the Marshalls. I had eight brothers and five sisters. 'You don't want to go down that street, that's the Marshalls' street.' At the back of Kiwi Street, there was a big oval called Warren Park. All the families used to meet there to have a big game of soccer, which would then become rugby league. And it got very physical. I think Benji was lucky to have all his uncles around. We all have different personalities, so we had a lot to offer him.

I was the protective one. Because he was named after me, I used to always comfort him, while my older brothers would give him a hard time. Because I was the youngest boy, my brothers would always shield me from trouble, and I tried to give Benji that same guidance.

Whakatane is a beautiful town. The bush, the mountains and the coast are all within about 20 minutes of each other. I used to take Benji fishing. We would take a mate's boat out to a spot called Whale Island, about 7 km off Whakatane. We'd fish for snapper, kingfish, kahawai. We'd just enjoy the sun, we'd swim, we'd snorkel . . . and relax. Most weekends, we'd be out there. At others times I'd throw him on the four-wheeler and take him down to the beach.

He was fairly level-headed when he was younger. He would play touch football with all his uncles — everybody claims to have taught him the flick pass or the long ball. 'He must have learnt that one off me.'

Because he was used to playing with adults, he was always mature

GOD DEFEND ME

for his age. I remember him playing for the New Zealand under-21s touch football team when he was 16. To see a guy that young who was so mature just blew me away. He used to play for the First XV at rugby union and then play for my brother Phil's senior side afterwards. I never liked him doing that. Phil's side was full of cowboys who'd hit you from behind. I thought he'd get hurt, but he coped alright.

I'd take him here, I'd take him there, for his sport. He just got better and better at anything he turned his hand to. It was a joy for me to take him up and down the country on the way to and from events. He's come a long way.

But he was humble. When he was 13, he was playing for the Bay of Plenty under-13s. I took him to Rotorua, where the side was playing against Auckland, considered the top team in the division. Benji wasn't even a regular in the team, but someone got hurt and he played that day. Benji's team won, and it was because of him. He had a perfect day. He had vision, which I put down to playing with older blokes. All the parents came up to him afterwards, saying: 'You won them that game.' He didn't think anything of it. It was just another game of footy.

In the same week he got the scholarship with Keebra Park on the Gold Coast, he was named in the New Zealand under-16 rugby union team. I was always worried he was going to hook up with the wrong blokes in Whakatane so I was quite comfortable with his mum's decision to send him to Australia. He had a lot of good mates who went down the wrong path, and some of them were very talented sportsmen. There can be a lot of jealousy in small towns occasionally. People, especially parents of other kids, don't always like to see others do well. I still think he could have made it either way. He could have been an All Black if he'd stayed. As long as he stayed on the right path.

My family is always telling me that I don't get enough credit for him. But I don't want credit. He knows who I am and I know who he is. I'm not after any fame or glory. I'm just happy to be a part of it. To see what he's done and what he's doing. What I've done, anybody would do for their kids.

Friends come and go, but families are there forever. His uncles are all so proud of him. He has opened up some doors for us. He always thanks us for bringing him up, but we can't thank him enough for what he's done for us.

Chapter 10

On Top of the World

THE TIGERS failed to reach the finals in 2008. It got worse for me, too; if your team didn't make the finals, and you were named in the New Zealand World Cup train-on squad, you trained. During that finals series of '08, we weren't just trained, we were flogged. Stephen Kearney was the new Kiwis coach and he brought a new culture and discipline into the squad from day one. Before he arrived, you could get away with some little lapses in discipline. Steve set down a number of rules. The first I came across was the pre-tournament torture.

We all expected the training to be fairly relaxed. And then in the first session, we were worked like I'd never been worked before. It continued for the four weeks of the finals. We were based at Parramatta. The Eels' trainer, Hayden Knowles, was part of our staff. He brought Rod 'Rocket' Reddy along for the ride and they set about working us into the ground. And then telling us to get up to do it all again.

The day before Labour Day — a day after the NRL grand final — I asked Hayden if we would be having the public holiday Monday off. He said: 'Don't you worry, you'll be training.' He wanted us to be training when he knew no one else would be. 'We're going to win this thing,' he would say to us.

I always liked to have a few beers while watching the grand final, but I couldn't, knowing I'd be training the next day. I was fortunate I didn't, as I arrived at training to be greeted by the words: 'Today is not for these boys, it's for you.'

All the forwards had to do the fitness session on the treadmills. Half of them would be on the treadmill and the other half would be in a circle, surrounding me on a large mat. I was standing in the middle of the mat while Hayden would call out the names: Nathan Cayless, David Fa'alogo, Roy Asotasi. When he called their name, they would run at me and I had to tackle them to the floor. It lasted about 45 minutes. And they didn't go soft on me. They were running their hardest. I was hurting. Back then, I still had some doubts about my ability to tackle, after all the injuries I'd had. But after that day, wrestling those big boys on a public holiday, many of those doubts disappeared.

IN THE first days of New Zealand camp, it is tradition for all the players to form a circle and tell your teammates what it means for you to be in the team, for you to be among them. Ruben Wiki started it.

You would stand in front of all of your teammates, introduce yourself and bare your soul. On the first day of World Cup camp, I stood up and told my teammates words to the effect of: 'It's an honour and a privilege to be playing with you. I've missed out on my fair share of games for the Kiwis, and in the World Cup I want to make a difference. I know my tackling hasn't been the best over the past few years but I am going to do everything I can during and after training to make sure my defence is up to standard. I will prove it to you. I'm going to prove to you I'm not going to let anyone down.'

Afterwards, Wayne Bennett, who was an assistant coach to Steve, approached me and said: 'One of the hardest things to do is to admit your weakness to your team. For you to say that in front of them meant a lot to them.' I didn't do it for that reason. I did it because I wanted my teammates to know I was going to do everything I could to win that World Cup.

Ruben told me he'd help me. After every session, I would do tackle practice, mostly with Ruben but also David Kidwell, Nathan Cayless and others. While some of the other guys would kick goals or muck around, I'd tackle the big blokes. They would get stuck right into me, working up a full steam, and I'd have to take them down. They taught me a few different techniques as well. But most importantly, by the time the first game came around, my confidence was returning. I knew that I'd spent most days tackling those big blokes, so I could handle anything that was thrown my way. If I missed one or two during a game, Ruben would run on and tell me to put my body on the line. I'd never want Ruben to think I was soft, so I would.

I was on such a high. I had never trained that hard in my life, and never tackled so many blokes who were so big, on so many occasions. There was a bit of pressure on me through the tournament. Sonny Bill Williams had quit the sport, so a lot of the headlines revolved around me. But I was ready. In the back of my mind, I knew that any more shoulder problems would probably end my career. But at the same time, something wonderful was happening. I started to forget about those dodgy joints and just tackle.

PRIOR TO the tournament proper, I achieved one of the highlights of my career. I played with Stacey Jones. When I knew

Stacey was retiring, I thought I had missed my chance. So when the All Golds side, which was playing against NZ Maori in New Plymouth, was selected, I was always keen to play, knowing Stacey would be. Training with him before that game, I felt like a little kid. I'm usually quite loud and boisterous, but in this particular camp I just sat back and watched, in awe of the bloke. I tried to talk to him as much as I could and soak it all up. It was a learning experience for me, to see how the master prepared and played.

He was the only reason I watched the Warriors as a kid growing up in New Zealand. He was the reason I enjoyed watching rugby league. I could have sat that game out if I had wanted to, but it was a dream for me to play with Stacey. I was never going to miss that opportunity. I was able to tick off one of the most important goals of my career.

WE WERE poor in our first match of the World Cup tournament, against Australia. We trialled well against Tonga, and we were confident. We had depth and we were as fit as any Kiwi squad I could recall. But we couldn't put it together against the Aussies at the Sydney Football Stadium. We scored first then the Aussies scored the last 30. It was disappointing. Steve told us we dogged it and it was difficult to disagree with him. From there, we travelled to the Gold Coast to play Papua New Guinea. We had a good week and we won comfortably. I set up a few tries in the first half and with my hamstring playing up a bit, Steve told me to rest up in the second half. I just iced up the hamstring on the sidelines.

The next day, the newspapers had me being in doubt to play England in Newcastle the following week. We decided to play a bit of a joke. When the media was around at the start of our training sessions, I wouldn't take part. I'd be doing hamstring work, trying to give the impression that I wouldn't be right for the game. Then when the media left I'd jump straight into the training session. I was always going to play. I was never going to miss that game because Steve asked me to captain my country.

We knew, regardless of the result, we would be playing England a week later in the semi-final, so Steve named a few of the fringe players in the squad. He left our skipper Nathan Cayless out. At the beginning of the week, Steve came up to me and said: 'I think you're captain material for the team, and I want to name you captain of the team. What do you think about that?' What did I think? Well, I told him Jeremy Smith was in the side, so was David Kidwell, and both would make great captains. It was hard to say yes at first. But I knew he must have asked me for a reason. I could tell he wasn't joking. I'd been captain at school, at the Tigers . . . it was the proudest day of my international career, being told I was going to captain my country. I always wanted to play for New Zealand and had obviously dreamed of being captain, but to get the chance to actually do it, in a World Cup against England no less, was difficult to believe. I ran onto the field a little teary, from the front, moving to the head of the line for the anthems.

I had always remembered that Ruben Wiki, when captain, used to put his fist on his chest, because he only had one arm around a teammate. I didn't know what to do with my spare hand. I started off with it by my side, but eventually, all caught up in the emotion, it ended up on my heart.

JUST PRIOR to the game, the English did one of the most disrespectful things I've seen on a football field. They stayed in a huddle during the haka and would not face us. Just before we started it, our hooker Issac Luke said: 'Let's walk towards them.' We did. They just stayed there, in their huddle, and wouldn't even look at us. I asked their second rower Gareth Ellis about it later and he said he felt embarrassed, but the team was told to do it.

They wanted a reaction and they got one. If they wouldn't face us, we'd go to them. We were on their 40-metre line and we all stood right in front of their huddle and unleashed some serious fury. We huddled up ourselves afterwards and I said to the boys: 'If they want to disrespect us like that, let's go out there and give it to them.' The emotion really took over. We were fired up and we ended up beating them fairly comfortably.

SO IT was England again, this time in Brisbane, which was a little difficult to prepare for as we had only just played them. We changed the team around a bit, but we made sure we stuck to the same routine.

We would train lightly earlier in the week, and then lift the intensity. On Wednesday nights, we would also have a family dinner. Everyone would bring their families, some of whom were touring with them. Steve and Nathan would get up and say a few words to them, thanking them for their support. We could break camp for the night and stay with our families if we wanted to, making sure we returned for training on Thursday afternoon.

Wayne was taking care of our defence, while Steve took charge of our attack. They had a great system set up in the coaching department. Everything was set up to make sure everyone had a job to do, and we all knew exactly what our job was. It ran like clockwork.

Action Photographics

Left: Friendly fire; in round eight of 2007, not long after Taniela Tuiaki clattered into me as I tackled Israel Folau. I suffered a fractured shoulder. It was the most painful of all my shoulder injuries.

Below: Nowhere to hide; I can't escape the cameras even on the sideline.

Action Photographics

Action Photographics

Stalking the Cowboys at Leichhardt Oval, 30 July 2007.

Action Photographics

With my long-time club coach Tim Sheens. I can generally predict what he is going to say, but that doesn't mean I don't listen to him.

In the Foundation Cup trial against Sydney Roosters at the SFS, 2008.

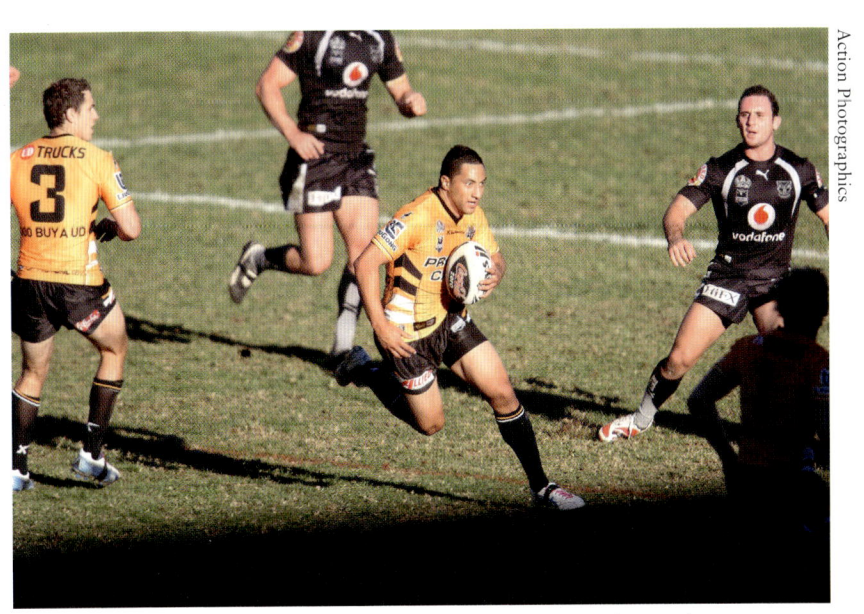

Mate against mate; opposing my Kiwi teammate Lance Hohaia, who was playing for the Warriors, at Leichhardt Oval, 29 June 2008.

Action Photographics

Celebrating a try with Chris Heighington against the Bulldogs on 3 August 2008.

Firing one out wide against Penrith, 4 April 2009.

Action Photographics

Just give me the ball; round two, 2010, against the Roosters.

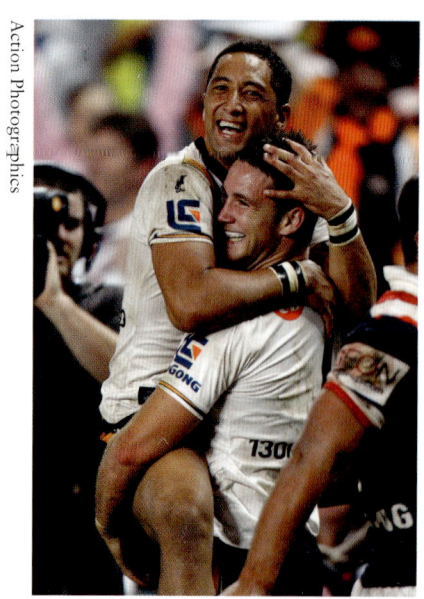

With my good mate Tim Moltzen against the Roosters.

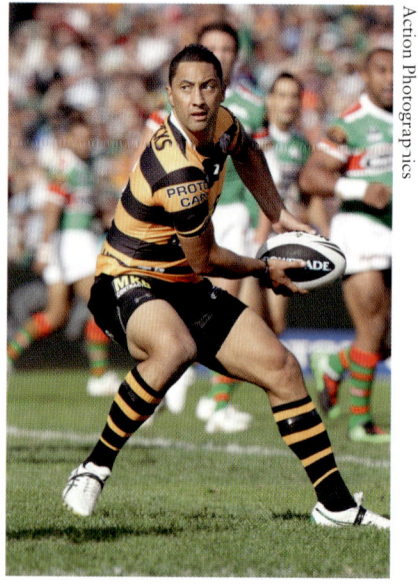

At the grand old Sydney Cricket Ground, playing South Sydney, on 16 May 2010. Unfortunately, it wasn't a grand occasion for us; we lost 50–10.

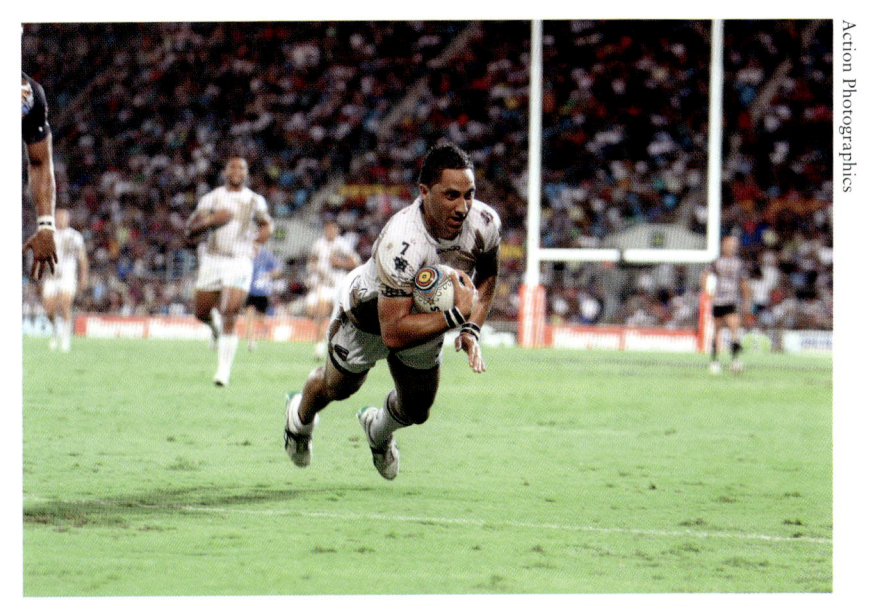

Diving over for a try in the inaugural All Stars game on the Gold Coast, 13 February 2010.

At the pre-game press conference the following year, with Nathan Hindmarsh to my left and Wayne Bennett to my right. Wayne looks impressed with the question.

Launching the NRL season at Casula, 2 March 2011.

On the way to a try against the Warriors at Mt Smart Stadium, round 14, 2011.

I liked Wayne Bennett straight away, and I think he liked me. The World Cup camp was the first time I had met him in any great depth. He knew I was a bit of a character and I immediately started to test the boundaries. I called him 'long neck' and 'giraffe'. I told him I'd take the coat hanger out of his shirt. He got into me immediately so I felt comfortable giving it back. It made the boys relax a bit, I think. Away from coaching, Wayne believes he's just about the funniest guy in the world. I can certainly say that he is vastly different to the persona that many people see, just about the opposite. When it comes to football he is serious. But away from it . . . whenever there was dinner on during camp, everyone would know I'd be sitting next to Wayne. What I like about him is that he tells you what you need to hear. If you play a bad game, he's not going to tell you that you played well. If you play well, he's still not going to tell you that you played well. That's what you need to hear in football sometimes. He never sugar-coats anything. If you stuff up, he will make sure you don't do it again.

Against the English in the semi-final, we didn't produce our best performance. We got away with the game in the end, winning 32–22. By this stage I had become very close with Wayne.

I had grown to know by this stage that when Wayne wouldn't speak to me, it clearly meant he was angry with me. After the semi-final, he walked around the dressing room, talking to each of the players individually, telling them they did this well or that well. I was sitting in the ice bath with Lance Hohaia, looking at Wayne. He wouldn't even look at us. We had made a few mistakes, and it was clear that he was filthy at both of us. I didn't know what to do under the circumstances. Eventually, I decided: 'Right, if he's not going to talk to me, I'm not going to talk to him.'

After the game, we were allowed a few days off to see family. We all returned and I saw Wayne and said: 'Are you over your little tantrum yet?' In front of the whole team. He said: 'As a matter of fact, Benji, I am, but you still played like shit.' We had a big hug in front of the whole team. I said: 'That's all you had to say, instead of avoiding me for an hour.'

Steve used to take care of the technical side of things, the video work, the game plan and tip sheets, all the tireless and possibly thankless stuff. Wayne tried to coach each player individually. He used wonderful analogies to put his point across. And he has an incredible ability to stir you up for a big game. Some of what he said gave me goosebumps. He had the whole room hanging on every word. It's not so much what he says, but the way he says it; the tone he uses. He made everyone feel like they were desperate to play for each other. Anyone who has been coached by Wayne Bennett will know what I'm talking about; there is a lot of pausing, to give you time to soak in what he has just said, and a lot of repetition.

IT WAS my first ever tour with the national side, and I was lapping it up. I was playing solidly, and I wasn't worried about my shoulders. But a lot of other people were. There was plenty of pressure on me from the media.

On the Friday morning before the final, Wayne showed me a newspaper, which detailed a 'Bash Benji' campaign. I told him I didn't read the papers before games. He said: 'Read it.' It suggested that I was driven by fear, and stated the Aussies were going to try to bash me. He said to me: 'How does that make you feel?' I said: 'It makes me angry, but they can bash me if they want.' He said: 'They've got to catch you first.' It really did rile me. For much of the week, the talk had been about whether I would handle the pressure, whether my shoulders would handle the strain.

I actually thought I'd tackled well throughout the tournament. That day at training, I was filthy. Ruben said to me: 'What's wrong with you?' I was putting everything I had into the session, into the tackling pads. He liked it. He started running harder at me, so I'd try to hit harder.

I did take that anger into the game. The Australians were sledging me, but I enjoyed that. 'Run at Marshall,' they'd say, spotting me in the defensive line. 'There he is,' they'd say, pointing at me. I'd been put under pressure like that many times previously. I just had to handle it.

I didn't start well, mind you. Nathan Fien put a grubber through inside the first 10 minutes and I dropped the ball over the line. Australia scored twice not long after, through Darren Lockyer and David Williams. We were fortunate we weren't 18–0 down; Darren dropped the ball over the line himself.

We hit back through Jeremy Smith, then Jerome Ropati scored after Anthony Laffranchi was ruled to have stripped the ball from me — I'd like to think it was just a good offload! We weren't playing well but we were still in the contest. At that stage, we had a great sense of belief in the squad.

Wayne's speech to us before the game was good, but his talk at halftime was something else. I felt like a boxer, ready to go out for a heavyweight fight. That said, I don't wish to downplay what Steve did to that team. Wayne was important, but Stephen Kearney was the key. He changed the culture of our squad. He knew how to get the best out of his players, and he could relate to the Polynesian players. He also knew who to kick in the arse, and who needed to be dealt with a little softer. He had shown clips of Kiwi teams from the past, competing for 20 minutes and then falling away. At halftime of that final, we knew exactly what we needed to do. We wouldn't be falling away.

The Aussies seemed to be reading from our script. They started making mistakes. I guess the best example of that was Billy Slater throwing the ball infield, which allowed me to score in the corner. I'd never seen Billy do anything like that before, but they were under pressure. They hadn't been under that sort of pressure all tournament, and they cracked. It was one of New Zealand's greatest wins. To see the look on the faces of the Australian players . . . I knew it well; it was the look we were used to. That was the first time I had beaten Australia. I looked at them and thought: 'Is that what we look like?'

They were devastated. We celebrated. We did a lap of honour, and gave an impromptu haka to our families. In the sheds, we started skolling beer out of the trophy. Steve addressed the team, as did Wayne and Nathan Cayless. There were a few tears. We all posed for photographs with the trophy. I'd won a premiership before and I was feeling the same emotions. New Zealand teams hadn't had that sort of success for a long time. We had been given two jumpers for the game and, with many of us not changing at halftime, we put our fresh ones on.

We were driven back to the team hotel, where there were hundreds of people waiting for us: family, friends and supporters. They made a tunnel for us to walk through into the hotel. We had some dinner and Steve told us not to put a blotch on the win by doing anything stupid. All of our hotels had given positive feedback about us. We were a professional team, which meant no mistakes off the field as well as on it. The little things that some people wouldn't appreciate were important to us; no thongs or singlets at dinner, always closed shoes. We all stayed at the hotel that night, with our families.

THE EMPHASIS on discipline meant we had built up a substantial fine kitty. We took it all to the Normanby Hotel the next day. Some of the team had to go back to New Zealand, but most of us went to the pub. About an hour into our morning after the night before celebrations, the Australians turned up. A few of them, clearly still devastated, didn't acknowledge us, but I clearly remember Petero Civoniceva sitting down with us and congratulating us.

I can honestly say, he and my Tigers teammate Gareth Ellis are the nicest men I've ever come across in the game. Petero told us: 'You know what, I thought during the game you guys were going to give up, but you took it to another level.' He had several beers with us and a few of the Aussies joined in eventually. I realise it would have been strange for them.

At one stage, on the television in the pub, up popped Manu Vatuvei and Jerome Ropati, two of the boys who had flown back to Auckland. They were filmed with the trophy at the airport, with what looked like thousands of supporters cheering them. We skolled drinks watching footage of our teammates raising the trophy at the airport. It was priceless.

Quit and run

WHEN I was a kid, I didn't want to be Benji Marshall. I wanted to be Justin Marshall. I loved rugby union, and growing up all I wanted to be was an All Black. I never, ever, considered the possibility that I would be playing rugby league for my country. I wanted to be an All Black, plain and simple. That was every kid's dream where I grew up. I used to live rugby. I used to pretend I was Justin Marshall, because we shared the same surname and because he was a halfback. I used to play halfback when I was younger.

I also represented Bay of Plenty in rugby union, progressing to the New Zealand under-15s rugby union side.

My family also had a history in the sport. My dad, Mick, had played rugby union for Bay of Plenty. He played against the British Lions in 1966. He never used to talk about himself. When he used to give me advice, it was never a response to what he did as a sportsman. It was always about everyone else with Dad, and much of the time it was about me. My mum used to tell me about his career more than he did. He had an All Blacks trial at one stage.

He was a winger. He was fast and could kick goals. His mates would tell me stories about him. His life was rugby union until I started playing league. Most conversations with him would include a reference to how the All Blacks were faring, or Bay of Plenty.

Fate took me to rugby league, but I almost went back.

Early in my career, there had been some talk of interest from the New Zealand rugby union. If it became anything more than a slight interest, no one ever told me. I was invited to a Bledisloe Cup game in Sydney by the New Zealand Rugby Union, and there were suggestions I was being courted by them. At the time, I just thought they were being nice. Maybe I was naive.

It wasn't until early in 2009, just a few months after the World Cup victory, that I ever really considered switching. Actually, switching is not really the correct term. It was more an affair than a second marriage. Once I started playing league, I never really wanted to play rugby until an opportunity appeared to play in Japan. It was something I strongly considered. Many people dismissed the option of playing a stint in Japan as a publicity stunt, but I can honestly say I seriously considered the move.

I was off contract at the end of 2009 and there were still doubts about me given all the injuries I had suffered. My manager, Martin Tauber, received an email, out of the blue, from an agent in Japan claiming a couple of rugby union clubs were interested in me. I just had to be there from November until March. I could have earned about A$800,000 for some 14 games.

We ran it by Wests Tigers, and the officials there were open to the idea. It would provide them salary cap relief, as the club wouldn't have to pay me as much for my next contract because I could earn so much in Japan. It would just mean me playing out my contract with the Tigers until the end of the 2009 season, heading to Japan for the stint and then signing a new contract with the Tigers on my return. I would be staying fit over there. There weren't many negatives, we thought. Tim Sheens thought it was a great idea.

But David Gallop, the NRL chief executive, didn't. Just as I was about to fly over with Martin to have a look at some of the facilities, he said he wouldn't allow it. He said if I did do it I wouldn't be welcomed back to league.

I just couldn't work that one out, knowing that Mat Rogers and Lote Tuqiri were both welcomed back. It was pretty disappointing, and I was quite angry with David Gallop at the time.

It is still something I might consider one day. But I must say, having sat down and thought about it since, I know that while it would have been a great experience, I probably would have been doing it for the wrong reasons.

I could have quit the game completely. And don't believe that I wasn't serious about that. It was the only time I really considered leaving the Tigers. I wouldn't want to play for any other team in the NRL, so it was either change codes or stay with the Tigers. My mind was telling me to crunch the numbers and go, but my heart was telling me to stay.

I'm happy I followed my heart. I really felt I owed the Tigers something by staying. They had stuck by me through all my injuries, and they were still paying me reasonably good money considering the number of games I had missed. I felt I had to give something back. I don't think I could have looked my teammates in the eye and told them I was leaving.

Having more money wasn't going to make me any happier. And it wouldn't have made my football any better. I would have been thrust into the unknown, not to mention eating something I don't like — raw fish. It will probably be forever a case of 'what could have been'. I think I could have been good at rugby union. But it didn't happen. In all likelihood, it won't.

Chapter 11

Dad

THE FIRST time I had an inkling something was wrong was in Rotorua, before the Four Nations in 2009. We were playing a trial against Tonga there.

Much of my family had come to watch. After the game, back at the team hotel, Paula — Mick and Annalie's daughter — said to me: 'Do you think Dad looks a bit sick?' I hadn't really noticed. I told her I didn't. She said: 'He's been a bit sick lately.' 'What do you mean?' I replied. 'Just not feeling well,' she said. Later I said to him: 'You alright?' He said he was. So I left for the UK not thinking any more of it.

Unbeknown to me, while I was away, Mick fell while he was fixing a fence on the farm and landed on his stomach. He had an x-ray at the hospital, and the doctors discovered he had pancreatic cancer.

He might not have known until the very end if he had not fallen that day. He wouldn't have told anyone if he was hurting because he would not have wanted to create a fuss. He would have just gotten sicker.

The doctors told him they didn't know how long he had left, but that he might deteriorate quickly. He could have chemotherapy, which would prolong his life, or he could let nature take its course.

I had just returned from the Four Nations when my Uncle Bensy informed me. The cancer had been discovered while I was in England but no one told me. They thought I would have returned home. They were right about that. I would have. Bensy told me he wanted to get a coffee with me. He doesn't drink a lot of coffee, so I knew something was wrong. The last occasion he asked me to get a coffee with him, he told me my Aunty Mary had passed away. He explained what had happened. 'Your old man's sick,' he said. 'Sick?' I said. 'Yeah, cancer.' I started crying. 'How long's it been?' I asked. 'Three or four weeks,' Bensy told me.

I telephoned him straight away. I cannot remember who answered, but I gave them a gobful for not telling me when they all knew. I was filthy. The old man got on the phone like nothing had happened. 'Hello,' he said. I couldn't even talk to him. He was dying of cancer and he was talking like nothing had happened. I was on the phone to him for about 10 minutes, stalking the street over the road from my local café, and I hardly said a word.

'Don't worry about me,' he'd say. 'I'm alright. How was England?'

How was England?! I kept crying. I was trying to speak, but my mouth just failed me. The one thing I did say to him was, 'I'm sorry.' I quickly spoke to Mum, but she was struggling to talk as well. She put her other daughter Nicola on. Nicola explained everything. *Pancreatic cancer. They don't know how long it'll be. He's losing a lot of weight and getting sicker.*

She also explained the options; chemo or let the cancer take him. I said: 'You tell him to do whatever it takes to live longer.' I didn't understand then that it would just mean prolonging the pain. I didn't want to understand it.

DAD

BENSY BOOKED me on the first flight he could to get me out of Sydney to Auckland. As he did, I packed my bags. I left later that day.

The driveway at Mum and Dad's place is a long one. Nicola picked me up from the airport in Whakatane and she told me my dad was in good spirits. I was pretending that I was okay, but I wasn't. I started to realise that as we drove up the driveway. By the time we arrived at the house, I couldn't even get out of the car. I just sat there crying.

Nicola went inside and told everyone I wouldn't, or couldn't, come in. Mum came out, followed by the old man. He looked bloated where the cancer was. I could still hardly speak. I gave him a hug and didn't let go for about five minutes. I look back now and think that I was more shattered at that moment than when he actually passed away. When he died, there was an inevitability to it. I knew it was going to happen. When I held him that day, the emotions were still very raw. I didn't know how I was going to feel about it until I actually saw him. I took my bags into my room and sat in there for about an hour. Dad had to come in and fetch me, telling me to come out. The worst part was that the rest of my family had already come to grips with it, as much as they could, but then I started it all again. Dad was the only one not crying.

EVERY YEAR, I try to play in the State Cup touch football tournament in Port Macquarie, on the first weekend in December. Usually, I would play that competition and then go back to New Zealand after it finished, to spend Christmas with my family.

Dad's illness had all happened prior to the tournament. I had planned to stay with my dad. I didn't leave the house and I tried to spend every moment with him. After a few days you get past the sadness and try to be happy. But every day, he'd be a bit more tired. He was the type of person who would never stay in his room during the day ordinarily, and he'd never rise after 7 a.m. I knew he was sick because I'd be getting up at 7 o'clock, wanting to spend the morning with him, and I wouldn't see him until 10 a.m. or later.

He had decided against chemotherapy. I argued with my family about it after I arrived but, ultimately, it was his decision. He had seen his sisters go through chemo and he didn't want to put up with that sort of pain.

When visitors came over, he would pretend like nothing was wrong and put on a brave face. I couldn't handle that. He was in so much pain and on so many different drugs, but he was still somehow upbeat. When the visitors left the house he would be back in bed in agony.

Around that time, I was nominated for two Maori Sports Awards, sportsman of the year and overall sportsperson of the year. The awards clashed with the touch tournament. I originally told Dad I would not go to Port Macquarie, but he told me he was okay. 'Book your flight for Wednesday and come back next week.' I had previously committed to the touch tournament, so I phoned the organisers of the awards and told them I wouldn't be able to attend their function. They told me I had won two awards. Eventually, we decided that I would record a video message. I did so for both awards.

On the Wednesday I was due to fly out, I woke at about 6 a.m. to the sound of clanging cups and pans from the kitchen. I thought there was no way it would be Dad making all that noise. Sure enough, when I got up he was in the sunroom, sitting on his chair waiting for me.

DAD

I sat down with him. Mum must have known that he wanted to spend time with me because she stayed in bed. We talked for hours. I told him then that I'd been nominated for the Maori Sports Awards. He told me I should go. I could tell he really wanted me to go to the awards.

I also told him then that when I retired, I wanted to start a charity. He said to me: 'Why wait till you retire? You've got the profile in the game now. Do it now.' He went on: 'There're two things I want you to do. I want you to always look after your family, and use your profile to help kids. It's close to you, and you can make a difference.' It was a dying man's wish. What was I to say?

I had always wanted to help people, I just didn't know how. When Dad said that, it all made sense to me. Cancer is in my family. We've lost my grandmother, Kahira, and Aunty Mary, both to breast cancer, my Aunty Judith to bowel cancer. An uncle and a cousin have beaten it. It's not easy to see anyone go through cancer, but it's harder to see kids go through it. All the children's hospitals I've been to have had an effect on me, seeing the looks on the kids' faces when we visit them. I wanted to help in a bigger way. And I can. What Dad said made sense. What was the point of waiting?

That morning, Dad and I also spoke about playing, and pressure. I told him I felt like quitting sometimes. He said: 'Don't give up, don't give up. It's just a sport. If it's taking too much of a toll on your life, you don't have to do it, but don't give up just because things are getting too hard.'

Then I said to him: 'Why are we talking about this anyway? I'll see you on Monday.' He said: 'Yeah, I just want to make sure you know.' I think he knew that he wasn't far away.

I RECALL giving my first Wests Tigers jersey, framed and embroidered with my name, date and the result, to Mick and Annalie as a Christmas present the year I debuted. They both cried when I handed it to them. It's still hanging up in their house, near my Australian Schoolboys jumper, and my second Test jersey. I started giving my awards and trophies to them. Dad made a trophy cabinet. They date back to Keebra Park: my sportsman of the year award from there.

Everything is still there. I leave it there because it's my home. When I go home I stay in the same room I grew up in. Mum makes me the same favourite meals that I like: deep-fried chicken schnitzel, with chips, salad and a homemade mayonnaise for dinner, and an egg, bacon and potato concoction for breakfast.

Dad would take all the visitors to the cabinet and show them all the trophies. He would make particular mention of the international five-eighth of the year award, which I won in 2009. Then he would sit them through all the books of newspaper clippings that Mum had put together. Even in his final days, he was showing people that cabinet, and what was inside it. They came to see him because he was sick and he'd just take them to show off the trophies.

Nicola phoned me every day while I was in Port Macquarie. She told me he was staying in bed longer and the brave face was starting to disappear. It was like he'd planned everything. I'd call him and he'd just say: 'I'm fine, boy.' Nicola would tell me the truth.

On Friday, she called to tell me he'd been rushed to hospital. She told me she thought I should come home. But he took the phone and said: 'Don't come home. It's okay, it's okay.' 'Are you sure?' 'Yeah, it's okay.' 'I love you. Bye.'

Stupid me. I believed him. It wouldn't have mattered in the

DAD

end. I wouldn't have made it home in time. I was told that at the hospital, some of my family sang and played the guitar for him. All of his favourite songs. While I was playing a game he apparently deteriorated. He'd asked for the priest. The family was sitting in the hospital room with him, holding hands.

Bensy was with me in Port Macquarie. He received the call from Michelle on the Friday, telling him Mick had died. I didn't really cry, because I had been home and grieved already. I told the boys I'd have to return home and why. I couldn't get a flight out of Port Macquarie until about 2 p.m. the next day, Saturday.

I had an idea. I phoned someone from the Maori Sports Awards. I said there was a chance I could attend the function, which was that night. Dad wanted me to go and I could only fly from Sydney to Auckland, not Whakatane. I wouldn't have been able to fly from Auckland to Whakatane until the Sunday. I could hire a car or I could do what Dad wanted. I asked her if there was anything she could do to get me out of Port Macquarie and over to Auckland.

Someone phoned Qantas, told them what had happened, and I was booked on the flight I originally could not get on, from Port Macquarie to Sydney. I assume I was given a standby seat. I had 45 minutes to get from Sydney's domestic terminal to the international flight. I was 15 minutes late, but Qantas held the flight open. When I walked on the plane, the flight attendant said to me: 'I'm sorry for your loss.' Even the pilots knew, apparently.

I arrived in Auckland about 4 p.m. The Sports Awards were at six o'clock. I was given a suit, shirt and bow tie. I arrived at the awards at 6.30 p.m. I knew I had won both the awards, so I was thinking to myself about what I would say. I was just thinking: 'Whatever you do, don't cry.'

I was announced as the sportsman of the year winner. I walked up on stage, took the microphone and, of course, started crying. People there were clapping, thinking that I was crying because of the award. I said: 'I lost my father last night. I shouldn't really even be here. But it's because of him that I am.'

At the end of the night, it was time for the big award, for sportsperson of the year. I walked up to the stage. Stan Walker, the Kiwi-born *Australian Idol* winner, was performing, and was meant to be closing the night with a song. Because he heard that my father had passed away, he wanted to perform a different one. He sang 'The Climb', by Miley Cyrus, and dedicated it to my dad. I lost it again. I gave a speech to the family back home in Whakatane.

I DIDN'T get much sleep that night, and I was booked on the first plane from Auckland to Whakatane in the morning. Up the driveway again . . . and everyone was waiting for me. I walked into the lounge room, and everyone just stared at me. The open coffin was positioned just near where my dad always sat in the room. I couldn't look at anyone. I lost it again. I sat down next to him and stayed there for the whole day. I hardly moved.

That night, the Maori Sports Awards were on television. So the family sat down and watched it, with my old man in the room. I didn't tell anyone what had happened or what I'd said. When I started crying during the awards night, the whole room followed. We watched while I dedicated the awards to Dad, and said hello to everyone sitting in the lounge room back home.

Then, we just started telling stories about the old man. I'm not sure what came over me, but I gave a speech to the family. I thanked them for accepting me into the family as their own, and I spoke of how it would have been easy for them to be jealous that

I'd taken Mum and Dad's attention. It was an amazing moment of reflection. I slept next to him that night, on the couch.

PEOPLE WOULD come and go over the next few days, paying their respects. And then who should show up at the front door? Tim Sheens, who had flown over with my manager Martin Tauber. That gave me enormous strength.

The hardest part of any grieving process, I believe, is the closing of the coffin. I was so happy that Tim was there to see that. Mum waited for him and Martin to arrive so they could be a part of it. Everyone got to say their final goodbyes, kiss the body, before they closed the lid for good.

I honestly don't think there would be many NRL coaches who would do what Tim did. I was so happy they were both there. Tim generally doesn't let players attend a family wedding if it means missing a training session, but he missed one himself to fly to Whakatane for me. I didn't know they were both coming until they turned up on the doorstep. Tim lifted everyone's spirits. People would come in and think: 'The Australian coach is here.'

Tim had lifted Dad's spirits in his final weeks, too. When I first returned to Whakatane after the Four Nations, I told Tim about him. He offered to help out where he could. They both loved talking about league, so I asked Tim to phone my dad, just to talk footy. It made his day. It made his life.

Those gestures meant more to me than anything Tim has done as a coach. For a long time I had a clause in my contract, which meant I could leave the Tigers if he did. If he did leave, I probably would have followed him. That's how much he means to me. He makes me want to play for him, and I don't want to let him down. He commands respect and he will always have mine.

MUM ASKED me to prepare a eulogy. I practised what I would say a hundred times, walking up and down the grass tennis court, which Dad took so much pride in. And I cried every time I did it.

But when it came to the real thing, I didn't. I think it was one of the best speeches I've delivered. Loud and honest and proud. I felt strong.

I didn't think there would ever have been as many people at the church as there were that day. The seating was extended at the back so that everyone could fit in. He was a popular and proud man and he deserved to have the place bursting. He got a fitting goodbye.

I do not regret not returning sooner from Port Macquarie. I got to say my own goodbye that Wednesday morning I spent with him in the sunroom. But he tricked me. He tricked me into thinking that everything was okay. When I left that day, I said: 'You'd better be here when I get back.' 'I'll be here.' I guess he was. He was still in the lounge room. He got me.

At the time, I didn't think much of that morning. But in hindsight, the signs were there. Why was he asking me to set up a charity? You can't say no to a dying man. Maybe he knew that and wanted to do some good.

The funny thing was, that morning he'd looked as good as he had over his final weeks. I thought later that it was as if he'd planned everything that way, so I'd make the awards and arrive home to watch them — with him.

He was always thinking of others. When he took me to hospital when I was a kid, after I'd broken my collarbone, he stayed with me for 12 hours and told stories about me to 20 or so people he didn't know. The whole family would say I was his pride and joy. He used to show me off to everyone. No one ever really told me that until he passed away.

DAD

I carried his photo with me throughout 2010. I had it with me for every game. That was the first year I didn't carry the photo of my brothers. They knew they had my support. Before the mid-year Test match in 2010, during the New Zealand national anthem, I cried thinking about him.

Annalie Doherty

I COULD have adopted Benjamin, but I never did because of Lydia, his mother. I also know that if I did adopt him, he would not be where he is today. I never would have let him go to Australia at the age he did. He was too young at 16, I thought. I hated seeing him go.

Mick and I would travel over to the Gold Coast to see him, to see how he was. He had a hard life over there. I almost brought him home on one occasion. If he had said to me, 'Mum, I want to come home,' I would have taken him, because I hated leaving him there. He was loved just as much as our own children.

But it must have been the best thing for him, because look at him now. I've often told him: 'If you had been with us, you wouldn't be where you are.' You never know, he might have played for the All Blacks. I'm sure he would have gone a long way. But he wouldn't be where he is.

Lydia was friendly with my second daughter, Nicola. They went to the same school and played in the same volleyball team. That's how I knew Lydia at first. When she was pregnant, Michelle was with Bensy but not married to him. When he was about six months old, Lydia asked Michelle if she'd mind looking after him. She was so young and she still had to have a life. So we babysat him. Then it became more frequent. I'd look after him overnight, then every weekend. I'd pick him up on Friday night and take him back on Monday morning.

If ever he was sick, he'd want to come home to us. Then when his mother moved to Edgecumbe, which was a little way out of town, he didn't want to go. We would have him during the week, and he would go to his mum's on weekends. I'd take him back to Lydia on Saturday and pick him up on Sunday. Then, he didn't want to leave on weekends. He wanted, I guess, a family life. I said to Benjamin: 'I really can't keep you.' We would have adopted him, but I couldn't take him off Lydia.

At first we just wanted to help Lydia out, but after a while we felt like he was just like our own. I can only recall him missing one Christmas at our house. He still comes home every year. I think last year was the first year I didn't bake him a birthday cake.

Mick and I had five children, Paula, Michelle, Nicola, Andrew and Troy, who were all still at home when he began to stay with us. Troy was 10 when we started looking after Benjamin. They became really close. Troy played with him all the time. They'd be playing outside and I'd say to Troy: 'Leave that poor kid alone. You won't be happy until you have him crying.' Sure enough . . .

But they all call him their brother. And he calls them his brothers and sisters. That's probably why he started to call us Mum and Dad. All our children did, so instead of being Nana, I was Mum. It's been like that ever since. I admire that about him. To all his friends, he calls me Mum, as well as Lydia. Lydia even says to him: 'There's your mum.' She's been so good through it all. She never, ever, stopped him coming out to me.

Everyone considered him one of ours, as well as Lydia's. On one particular day at school, when he was about five or six years old, Lydia was a little late collecting him, and the headmaster came out to see him and said: 'Who are you waiting for?' 'My mum,' he replied. 'Can I ring my mum and dad,' Benjamin added. 'Who's your dad?' the headmaster asked. He says: 'Mick Doherty.' Mick played squash with the headmaster. He said to Mick the next time they played: 'Have you got something to tell me? Who's this Benjamin Marshall that you're the father of?' We did cause some confusion on occasions.

DAD

Benjamin was a gorgeous kid, never naughty. I don't think I ever grounded him. He was a perfect little boy to bring up. And he had a lot of talent.

Mick was a great sportsman himself. He played rugby union successfully and he was also a good discus thrower. He used to always try to advise Benjamin. He used to teach him goal-kicking and tackling.

He idolised Benjamin. We had many of his medals and awards in a cabinet, and just before he died, I had to leave one of them, the international five-eighth of the year award, in the kitchen, because I was so sick of going to fetch it when people were visiting. He was so proud of him. We all were, but particularly Mick. It's very hard to visit Benjamin in Sydney without Mick, to see how well he is going. He would have just loved to see him progress.

That last morning he spent with Benjamin was so important. I think Mick had been waiting for that intimate occasion for quite a while. It was a beautiful father–son talk. I heard them talking from the bedroom, and when I did go out there, poor Benj was sobbing his heart out. I just bent over and put my arm around him. He spoke so beautifully at Mick's funeral. It would have meant so much to Mick. He's our family. For Mick, it was always: 'Benji, my boy.'

We never, ever thought we would be blessed with the pleasure that Benjamin has brought to us. He was just Benjamin Marshall to us. Mick and I were able to get over to Australia for a few Test matches, and of course the grand final. Actually, we came over for the previous game, just in case. If they didn't make the grand final, at least we had seen him in a final. We obviously couldn't go home then. It was such a moment. If he wins more of them, I just don't know if they could be as great as that first one, the way he played.

I am so proud of him, what he has done. I never miss a game. I watch every one, at home, on my own these days. Mick would have loved to have done what I am doing now, penning a few thoughts on Benji, who he loved so much. He's brought such great pleasure to our lives. Benjamin would ring me every week after his dad died, just to check how I was. I'm not his real mother, but he still classes me as his mum. I class him as my son.

Chapter 12

Iron Maiden

MY ONE true goal for 2010 was staring me in the face for a long time. Literally. For the whole season, it was in front of me every day.

Each year, Wests Tigers give out an 'Iron Man' award, for the player or players who have competed in every match of the season. Every year, I had either missed it by around 20 games, or just a handful. In 2005, I missed one game, the first one. Then came the years when I would be lucky to play a handful in one season. I was either incredibly close or distressingly far away. Both came with differing frustrations.

In 2010, I wanted that award bad. Every year from 2005 onwards I had set the same personal goal: win the Iron Man award. At the start of every year, every Wests Tigers player is asked to sit down and write our team goals as well as our individual ones. In 2010, I wanted to win the Four Nations and play every game of the NRL season. We are given folders to write in. Our goals are on the folders so we can be reminded of them every day. Tim also gives us stickers, and tells us to write our goals on them and stick them somewhere we can see them often. I put mine on the steering wheel of my car: 'Iron Man Award. Win Four Nations.' My two goals summed up in six words on my steering wheel. I'd pick people up and they'd look at me curiously. But I'd see the words every day.

There were games that year that I could easily have missed. There were games that year that I probably should have missed. Not many people truly get that side of rugby league. That's just what we do. Sometimes we play 50 percent fit. I've played just about on one leg before. I've played with one shoulder. I've had injections in my knee, or in my shoulder, just to take the field. My AC joint was actually playing up in a few games in 2010. You never quite seem to get enough time to let some injuries properly heal. So as soon as your AC joint cops another knock, it's out of whack again. You never tell anyone because you don't want the joint to be targeted.

There were times I thought I couldn't play, but then I'd remember my goal and I would just refuse to let whatever it was rule me out. After everything I've been through, no one knows my body like I do. I knew I could get through.

My immune system is generally dreadful when it comes to colds. But funnily enough, when I'm sick or hurting, I generally play better. I don't know why. There have been so many times when I'd be sick, and Tim Sheens would know very well how bad I felt, that the doctor had given me every pill under the sun to get me back out on the field after halftime, and I'd help win the game. You feel like you're going to die after it, but you just get through it.

I SHOULD never have played in the semi-final against Canberra. I'd been plagued by a knee injury during the week, which I suffered a week earlier against the Roosters. There is no way I should have played that night in Canberra. If it was a regular-season game, I wouldn't have played.

It was quite a bad one. The Roosters had made a little break, someone offloaded to Mitchell Pearce, and I came in to tackle him. His knee smashed into the side of my knee, and it felt like my knee buckled. I tried to get up and walk it off, but it wasn't cooperating.

Our trainer, Andrew Leeds, came on and said: 'We've got no interchanges left; you've got to stay on.' I tried to stay on, but I simply couldn't run. I tried to stay on the wing, but I felt like my knee was going to collapse.

Hobbling off the field and leaving my team short was one of the hardest things I have done. I felt like I was letting the team down. We had to play with 12 men for 10 minutes, until the beginning of extra time. And it proved costly. We should have won that game. It has been described as one of the best games ever, but I only see it as one of the worst. We were dominating the Roosters, and with 10 minutes to go I thought we still were. Then after I hurt my knee, and we were left with just 12 players, I had to sit there for 10 minutes and watch my team get destroyed. And there was nothing I could do. That hurt more than losing. I felt responsible and blamed myself.

No one blamed Chris Heighington, who lost the ball at the base of the scrum. He shouldn't have been packing into the scrum at lock. Robbie Farah usually does, but because I wasn't on the field, he had to feed the scrum. No one blamed Liam Fulton, who threw an intercept pass. He was shattered. But he was just trying to win the game. Not much was happening on the field and he was trying something. He was putting his hand up to win the game. I couldn't do that because I was watching it all from the sidelines. Everything happened because I wasn't on the field.

WE WERE still in the competition, though. Whether I was, however, was something else entirely.

I have a few friends who are physiotherapists. I play touch football with them. Long after the game, after I'd arrived home, one of them, Peter Moussa, brought an ice and compression machine over to my apartment. He sat with me through the night, for about six hours I would estimate, icing and compressing my knee. You're meant to implement the RICE regimen with injuries like that: rest, ice, compression and elevation. That machine let me do it all at once. He'd let me sleep and he'd let the machine do its work: 20 minutes on, 20 minutes off, for the whole night. Then he had to go to work in the morning.

He left the machine for me so I could use it during the day. Then he came back the next night. For three nights in a row, he did that for me. And if he didn't, I wouldn't have played the following week. At the start of the week, I was about a 20 percent chance of playing. The injury really did need time to heal. There was some bad bone bruising in there, as well as a strained ligament.

On the Wednesday, for our penultimate session, the media had packed Concord Oval out. Assistant coach Royce Simmons told me to stay inside while they were there and just do some passing with my teammate Gareth Ellis, who was in some doubt, too. I could run by then and few people knew.

I was in under the grandstands and the cameras were outside the doors, the lenses trained on me. I was limping around, pretending the damage was worse than it was. I knew by then I was going to be fit to play.

The team started doing some ballwork, and eventually the media left. Would you believe, we actually pretended we'd finished our training session. The team came off the field and gathered on the sideline. And when we were convinced that the media had gone, we trained again, in the rain, with me. It reminded me a little of when Patty Richards announced he was playing in the lead-up to the grand final. Tim didn't tell them I would be training that day. I wasn't sure myself until that afternoon, when I had a jog. That night, I watched the footage of me limping around on the news.

In Canberra, we were supposed to have a closed training session, but there were cameras behind bushes, behind fences, and they got footage of me running properly. We did a left versus right drill and I did a flick pass, which of course they showed on the news. Our ruse was over.

I quite enjoyed the whole charade, to be honest. It made me relax a bit.

Put simply, it was a massive effort to beat the Raiders in Canberra. Even when the crowds don't turn up, they are tough to beat on their own turf. But that night, the crowds turned up unlike anything else that year.

I always have a look at the other team during the warm-up. And I could tell they were nervous. They were dropping a couple of balls while everything we did was sticking. I felt I was at my best at that stage of that season, in terms of reading the game, and confidence. Just about every touch was a good one. I set up a few tries against Canberra; a flick pass to Chris Heighington, a no-look pass to Gareth for another. And we just hung on. My knee was so sore afterwards.

I had to do the same thing as I'd done a week earlier, icing and compressing my knee for three nights.

WE FELT confident of beating the Dragons. The hype around the game centred on it being a rematch of the 2005 preliminary final; redemption and revenge for them. We were confident. I'd never felt so confident.

It was a tough game. We were right in it; we scored first, then they did, then we did. I kicked the ball out on the full, then they scored. I dropped the ball, then they kicked a field goal. We lost. That about sums it up.

We had a chance to win it at the death. With a minute and a half remaining, we were down by one point, and I ran across to the left. They covered so I did some sort of pirouette, came back towards the right and threw a long ball to our prop Keith Galloway. He threw a dummy, made a break and sent the ball to our winger Beau Ryan. Beau chipped for Daniel Fitzhenry, but the Dragons hooker Dean Young got there first, when he had no right to. It was an amazing play by Dean. If he hadn't found himself there, we would have won the game.

I wasn't filthy after that game. I was dirty on myself for a few mistakes, but it was a successful season for the team and for me. It was, of course, disappointing not to reach the grand final, but we played for each other. And our results through the year reflected that. That's what we need to produce on a regular basis. The Dragons won the premiership by turning up for each other. Sometimes, we (and I'm very much included) try to play ourselves out of trouble instead of working our way out of trouble. We're starting to realise that now.

If we do the hard work, we know that our attack will match anyone's. If we tackle well, we win games. If we don't, we lose. We started to really find the balance that year, not pushing passes and taking the right options.

I was at the top of my game. Our forwards were going forward. They were relentless. And when we play like that, we're hard to beat.

We were disappointed after that game, but there was nothing we could do to change the result. I'd made a few mistakes, but you know what? When the game was on the line and we needed the points to win, I was still trying. I wanted to do something. I could have sulked, but I'm not like that. When games are on the line the boys look to me to do something. It almost came off.

You can't sulk. I touch the ball far more times than most players in the team. There are going to be errors here and there. There are errors around Johnathan Thurston's game, but he also touches the ball 80 or 90 times in a match. That's what halves do.

I'd be worried if I was only getting my hands on the ball 10 times in a game and making two or three mistakes. It's how I play — if the game is on the line, I want to be the one to stand up and win it for the team.

WE HAD made the finals for the first time since 2005. I didn't play a helluva lot of footy between those years, not as much as I wanted anyway. And we always seemed to be missing the finals by one or two points, one or two wins. That's when you look back at games you should have won earlier in the year, the matches that cost us finals spots. We tried to change that in 2010 and we did. We had to make the finals that year. It was long overdue. We fell to the eventual premiers by a point. That proves it was a successful year.

For me, it was a long and enjoyable year. It had begun with the All Stars game. That was a really enjoyable experience. It gave me the chance to play with some of the best players in the world. Playing with Darren Lockyer was unbelievable. I looked up to him when I was at school, before I played first grade. I wanted to be a five-eighth because of him and I wanted to play like him. To get the chance to play with him was a dream come true. I always wanted to do it but I never thought I'd have that opportunity. Then, of course, the year ended with the Four Nations, playing against those great players and winning.

That year represented the first time I had ever achieved the goals that I set at the start of the year. Receiving that Iron Man award was more pleasing, for me, than winning the Golden Boot, given what I'd been through to get it. It wouldn't have bothered me too much if I had missed out on the Golden Boot, even though I was extremely happy to win it. It was a huge surprise. But it would have been a successful enough season without winning it. It was the culmination of all the hard work that I'd done over the years. It is probably a miracle that I was able to get back to that sort of form.

Just to be on the field was an achievement, but to be playing some decent football . . . there were many times I'd doubted that I'd be putting my boots on, let alone winning the Golden Boot. I'm very proud of it. But I had never experienced the taste of playing every game, being injury-free, knowing that my shoulders or knees were not playing on my mind when all I wanted was to just play. I never thought I would be in that position. I was simply happy to be playing. I stood on stage, having received the Iron Man award at the end of the season, and said it was one of the most important awards I had ever received. I meant it.

Lleyton

I FIRST met Lleyton Giles at a training session at Concord Oval. I noticed a kid who had bandages on and had a cannula attached to his arm. His eyes were yellow and he looked lost. But as soon as he started hanging out with us, he found another gear.

Lleyton has been Wests Tigers' unofficial mascot since 2010, when I first met him. He has a condition called short-gut syndrome and doctors have told his family there is little they can do for him. He cannot store what he eats, so he needs a nutritional formula to survive. Over time, though, his liver will fail. He has been told that he cannot have a transplant — and he cannot be cured.

He led the team out against Penrith at Campbelltown Stadium during the regular season. I put him on my shoulders as we did a lap of honour after the game. All the players made a tunnel for him and he ran through it. Much of the crowd stayed to clap him off the field. He has been an inspiration to us.

His dad, Wes, said to me on one occasion: 'You don't know how much that means to us.' Then he broke down. He gave me a frame with four photographs of us with 'Benji My Hero' on it. At the end of the season, after we lost to St George Illawarra, I took him into the back room — because I knew I would cry. I gave him the jersey off my back and wrote on it: 'You're an inspiration to me.' At the same time, I was thinking of my dad, who had passed away less than a year earlier.

I said to his family: 'You don't know what you have done for me.' Lleyton's dad was crying. He has touched all the guys in the team.

We could have been dwelling on losing after that game. Everyone was disappointed, of course, but when Lleyton came in with a smile on his face, it was difficult to be too downcast. It was a football game. We lost, yes, but here was this boy who was fighting a far greater battle and still smiling.

His dad said we added six months to his life. What's more important; a game of football, or giving life to a boy?

Chapter 13

Four Nations

YOU DON'T often find triumph without the motivation of disappointment. The Kiwis' disappointment came through the 2009 Four Nations tournament. A year after our World Cup win, with a point to prove to everyone who might have felt that win was a fluke, we tanked, not even reaching the finals.

In 2009, I don't think we were as prepared as we were a year earlier. We just weren't on the job. We were more worried about what was happening away from football. We were getting fed up with a lot of things, including being away from home for a long stretch, the tournament being held in England and France. And we were all making way too many excuses.

I had learnt a lot from that year about being captain, especially in terms of leading by my actions rather than by what I say. I was the fulltime captain for the first time. I wasn't experienced. That tour taught me a lot of things about how I needed to act, and the things I needed to be doing that were right for a captain. It was a learning experience. I wasn't as confident as I should have been in the role, and I wasn't setting the right example. I'd have a beer on a Monday when there was nothing else to do. I was doing the little things that you think don't matter until you become more experienced in the role, and you realise the younger players are looking at what you're doing and following you.

In 2010, I felt I was ready to step up and be a *real* leader. I had a meeting with coach Stephen Kearney, who thought I wasn't getting my hands on the ball enough. Before we come into any camp with the Kiwis I always have a chat with him. We look at what worked previously and what didn't. We look at ways we can improve. We look at ways I can improve.

As a team, we also met. And we decided to get tough. Not just on our opponents but on ourselves. We came up with a lot of different rules. Everyone was just hungry again to win, especially after being so disappointed with what had occurred a year earlier. New plan, new discipline. There were plenty of fines, for tardiness, or breaking other rules. Players who weren't playing any given weekend were not allowed to drink during the week leading up to a game. It was one in, all in. The only time we could really have a drink was after our games, the plan being that it would be a celebratory one. Everyone had to prove to the team that they wanted to be in it.

We made sure everything we did was a sacrifice. If something is worth sacrificing your family for more than a month, it is certainly worth sacrificing a few beers during the week as well. There were a few rules broken in the first week, so we sat down and had another team meeting, to make sure everyone knew we were serious.

THE CAMP, and the campaign, began in Auckland, where we were playing a trial against Samoa. Steve rested the players who were involved in the NRL grand final, the Roosters and Dragons, and we just tried to get back into the swing of things.

The Samoans put together a good squad, which included a number of former Kiwi representatives like Tony Puletua, David Solomona, Ben Roberts, George Carmont and Ali Lauiti'iti. We thought they would be tough and they were.

They started off, truly, like they wanted to kill us. They were taking players out after they passed the ball, doing everything they could to get under our skin. That sort of aggression and intimidation was exactly what we needed. We beat them comfortably in the end but, physically, it was tough and it was hard. It was a good trial and it set the tone for the tour. We sat down afterwards and spoke about the fact that the rest of the tournament would be no different in terms of the physicality. The combinations that were so successful at the World Cup were working again: Lance Hohaia, Nathan Fien, Issac Luke and me. We were familiar with each other and everything seemed to be happening very smoothly early on.

I would sit down with those three other players before every game and run through what we were going to do. We made sure we all knew what the others' jobs were. If the four key playmakers knew what they were doing, hopefully the rest would follow. We travelled to Wellington for the first match of the tournament, against England at Westpac Stadium, or the Cake Tin. It was a Centenary Test, so we wore heritage jerseys. It was a significant occasion for us, and we broke the crowd record for a rugby league match in Wellington.

We knew the first game would likely determine whether it would be us or England who would play in the final against the Australians. If we lost to England, then Australia, we would be out. And having been bundled out before the final the previous year, we were desperate to ensure we at least made it to the last game of the tournament. The fact that England was the side which beat us 12 months earlier added to our motivation for the first-up game. We had a point to prove.

It was a challenge. They had what I thought was the best side they had put on a field in a long time, including my Tigers teammate Gareth Ellis as well as Sam Tomkins and Gareth Widdop. They took it to us in the first quarter. We had already been rocked by the loss of Manu Vatuvei inside the first three minutes, with a broken arm. Everything seemed to be going against us.

But we responded, and came away with the win. It was sweet revenge; they knocked us out in 2009, and we were hoping we could do exactly the same to them in 2010. And to be on home soil made the moment even sweeter, as we were so used to playing either in Australia or the UK. There are a lot of Kiwis in Australia, and we receive strong support from them, but it's just not the same as a game on New Zealand soil. The fact that it was Wellington, not Auckland, where we received such support was mind-blowing for me. I started to think that rugby league was really taking hold of people in the country. I regard it as one of the best crowds I've played in front of.

The next day, we travelled to Rotorua, where we would play Papua New Guinea. Rotorua is a real tourism hub, where people can see a lot of the history of New Zealand. It also has a lot of natural geysers, with a smell of sulphur that many can't handle. It's a big rugby league town, too, and we were welcomed like kings. We received a personal welcome home, like we were all coming back to a family reunion. It was good for some of the boys who might not have experienced that cultural side of the country before, or for a while at least.

It is also my local area, being in the Bay of Plenty. I felt like I was home for a while. Some of my family were following me, too, so I was able to spend a lot of time with them. We watched Australia play PNG on the Sunday on television. We were expecting Australia to win easily, but the Kumuls really bashed them. Menzie Yere, the centre nicknamed 'The Jukebox' (because he's got so many hits), was belting Darren Lockyer whenever he got near him. We couldn't believe it. They played like they hated the Australians, like they wanted to kill them.

We knew then that we would have a game on our hands the following weekend. Watching that game made us realise we had to focus. We couldn't simply run onto the field and expect to win. Sitting as a group watching the television, watching some of the best players in the world go black and blue with the tackles, set the tone for our week.

IN ENGLAND a year earlier, many of us had complained that we had nothing to do during the week. So with Rotorua being the capital of activities, we decided to take advantage. We did the luge, we went on the gondolas, and the town was also the venue for our go-karting finale.

We had decided that in the first few weeks of the tournament, we would go go-karting. And we would be playing for a championship. I consider myself a good driver and I was certainly confident. Jeremy Smith and Nathan Fien were the other two standout drivers of the group. When we raced it invariably became the three of us against each other, with the rest of the squad trying to take us out.

The first race had been in Auckland. Adam Blair was trying to wipe out anyone he could. The track staff had given us a big speech about not trying to wreck the karts and avoiding contact, and some of the big forwards were doing everything they could to break every rule in the place (what were we saying about following the rules?). I came second in Auckland and then again in Wellington, notwithstanding my new tactic of staying away from Adam Blair. We got to Rotorua and we found out we were racing what were meant to be the fastest go-karts in the world, with speeds of 100 kph. The track was 1.3 kilometres long. We thought, being a proper challenge, we would have a proper trophy. The New Zealand 'Stig' gave us a hand.

We were broken up into three groups for a qualifying session. The faster your lap, the closer up the front you would get for the start of the race proper. The Stig would start at the back and attempt to get round everyone. It took him until the last lap, but I think he was taking it easy. Of course, in the championship race, I finished second again.

At least I survived. We also took the opportunity to go white-water rafting in Rotorua. It was the day I thought I would drown.

We were told that the river on which we were about to set the rafts adrift included the biggest free-fall rapid in the southern hemisphere. Before we got to it, we navigated to the side of the river to be told we could get out and walk up the hill if we didn't feel comfortable with the big drop, or we could be a man and take it on. I'm scared of heights but some of my teammates were scared of water; they couldn't swim. The organisers explained that if the boat flipped, we were meant to hold onto the rope attached to the side of the raft. And if we couldn't, we weren't to panic; we had to curl up in a ball and the life jacket would float us to the surface. The water would feel like it's pulling you down, they said.

We didn't realise it at the time, but when the guides made a triangle sign with their hands, it was a signal to flip the boat. We were all in the raft thinking everything was okay, until all of a sudden the boat flipped. I was petrified. I held onto the side of the boat. I couldn't grab the rope. I thought I was gone.

I reckon I saw the light. Imagine it. 'Four Nations captain drowns.' I tried to curl into a ball, like we were told. We had been told not to panic. I panicked. I let the paddle go. I finally clambered back to the surface, grabbed the boat and was gasping for breath. The instructors were clearly a little worried. It was one of the scariest experiences I've had.

Other than that, we had a relaxed week. Steve and I turned up to a press conference prior to the game, with the PNG captain and coach, Stanley Gene and Paul Aiton. We outnumbered the reporters, so we had a fair idea what people thought about the game. We were a little disappointed. I kicked up a bit of a stink over it; we were taking the Kumuls seriously, but it appeared the local media was not. We played the game and, sure enough, the stories about 'The Jukebox' were all true. He was a big, hard dude and he came out of the line and took me out whenever he could when I didn't even have the ball. He flipped me over and then he said: 'Okay, you okay?' I said: 'Mate, you spear-tackled me on my head.' He replied: 'Sorry, sorry.' It ended up being a fairly one-sided contest. I think they had used up all their energy against the Australians.

WE HAD come up with a new haka for the tournament, and as we bussed to Auckland, instead of flying, I thought it would be a perfect opportunity for us to practise it. We went through the words about 30 or 40 times. We'd pull over and, by the side of the road, practise the actions. On that four-hour bus ride, we perfected our new haka, which had been created by the Maori coordinator who toured with us. It was our new one, it was a special one, and we wanted to get it right. A big part of touring is practising the haka, especially for the new guys.

During the week, we had a pre-arranged dinner with a number of Kiwi singers and bands. They sat down with their guitars and sang for us. It was a dress-up dinner for us. Each group had to pick a theme out of a hat and had a certain amount of money to spend on the outfits. Those amounts varied. My group was given 'super heroes'. There were cross-dressers and rock stars. Stephen Kearney's team won, dressing up as KISS.

Before the end of the night, after we had changed, we decided it would be a good opportunity to test out the new haka on the musicians; the first serious run-through, in the team room of the hotel. We blew them away.

We were playing against Australia at Eden Park, the spiritual home of New Zealand rugby union in Auckland. Both teams knew we would be meeting again the following week, but the match was a significant one for us. To get a chance to play a rugby league Test match there was overwhelming. We thought it was the ideal stage to throw the new haka at the Aussies.

Unfortunately, it took the focus off the actual playing of the game. We were prepared to play, but a lot of the emotion went into the new haka. Usually, we would practise it once or twice in the week before a game but on this occasion, we had five or six haka sessions.

We had spent so much emotional energy before the match even started; we ran out, then listened to the anthems, did our haka and then had to wait about five minutes before the match began. We were also embarrassed after the crowd booed the Australian national anthem. I'd never been a part of any sporting event where the home crowd booed the other's anthem. When the Australian anthem was being sung I couldn't help but feel embarrassed, and it was a little off-putting. I would later apologise for the behaviour. If our positions were reversed and our national anthem was booed, I would have been filthy.

We all ended the game feeling very down. Our performance was disappointing, especially as when we finally clicked, in the last 20 minutes, we dominated the Australians and showed a lot of promise. I set up a couple of tries with two flick passes. That 20 minutes did give us a lot of confidence. We knew we had never really put Australia under any great pressure — we also knew that the last time we did that, in the World Cup final, they had cracked. I told the team if we could just keep them under the pump and not let them get away to a start, we would give ourselves every chance.

As we sat down after the game and discussed what went wrong, a few of the boys made the point that we were too focused on making sure we knew the haka properly. It should not have been about that. We should be able to just do the haka and then go out and do our job on the field. It was a learning experience.

No one went out that night. We all stayed at the hotel together and made sure we were ready to travel. Our flight to Brisbane the next day was one of the quieter trips I have taken. Everyone was disappointed and embarrassed, especially given it was such a significant occasion.

We had a team meeting after we arrived in Brisbane, where everyone stated how they felt and what they wanted to achieve during the week. I said I just wanted to do my job. We decided to do the normal haka. We knew our job on the field and we knew the haka. Everyone knew that haka.

WHAT WE didn't know was that Wayne Bennett would be joining us again. Unbeknown to us all (I only found out just before he arrived), he addressed us on Friday, just before our final training session.

He just walked into the team meeting room, didn't say hello to anyone, and started talking. He hadn't met a lot of the guys in the team, and he just said: 'What was that shit last week? You call yourself the brotherhood — well you need to start acting like it.' He started asking questions of us. To Frank-Paul Nu'uausala: 'If your family was in trouble, would you do anything to help them?' 'Yep.' 'It's the same thing,' Wayne said. 'You call yourself a brotherhood, and last week you weren't doing anything to help each other at all.' It all just made sense. It hit home with a lot of the Islanders. I asked Wayne to come to our training session, but he thought it would create a media circus. He didn't want to take anything away from the work that Steve had done. Steve had done all the hard work. Wayne came in, said what he wanted to say, made everything make sense, and left. We got in the bus and went to training believing we could win.

We never really spoke about winning that week, mind you. All we talked about was not letting the Australians get away from us. We wanted to be in the contest at halftime and we were, at 6–all. We felt comfortable and we felt confident. But we went back out and they scored first. They led 12–6, but we still felt that we were grinding them down.

PEOPLE OFTEN ask me what it is like to play against a team that is coached by Tim Sheens. It is very weird. We don't speak for the whole week, as he thinks that will put me off my game. He started that tactic when he ignored me in his first game as Australian coach, in the 2009 mid-year Test (he wouldn't look at me during the build-up and he didn't even talk to me after the game). So I've played along ever since. I often think of my relationship with Tim as like a marriage. We have our good times and bad ones. But I can say that in the Four Nations final of 2010, I was actually helped by having him in the opposing coach's box.

Obviously, there's a flipside to that. But the thing is, he knows what I can do but he doesn't know what I'm going to do. I don't plan exactly what I'm going to do; I'll plan four things I could do. If I'm thinking I'll drop someone under me, I'll run across, and if the defender stops I won't give it to the player running under. But if he chases me too hard I will.

Over the past few years, Australian teams started to really chase me hard from the inside, thinking that I'd just run across-field. So I just started dropping it under and the tactic worked for us. It's easy to think what someone's going to do, but it's another thing to defend it.

Back in 2007, Tim asked Andrew Johns to do some coaching with me. It was a real buzz. I'd watched him so many times and I had admired the way he played. I like taking knowledge off everyone I can. I didn't employ everything he taught me, as some of it just didn't feel like me, but what I did use, I'm still using.

Joey taught me a lot of things during those seven or so sessions: why you should hold your hands up before you catch the ball, why tempo was important (going slow to trick the defence and then cutting to go fast), being up on your toes. They're things that I do naturally now, but I didn't back then. He also taught me his banana kicks, how to curve a ball in either direction.

In the Four Nations final, I received the ball following an offload in the second half. I was going to pass at first, but I knew the defensive structure employed by Tim Sheens and Peter Gentle, his assistant at the Tigers and with Australia. After offloads, they encourage you to come up and in from the outside to shut it down. I knew if I dummied they'd come up and in. So I tried it. I threw a dummy and no one moved. I threw another one and they started to move.

In the meantime, my winger Jason Nightingale was pointing to the ground, which is our signal for a kick. If I see him pointing to the ground I know he's ready to chase a kick. So I put it on the toe.

It was a kick which curved away, one of the very kicks I practised with Joey. It was bouncing further away from the fullback, Billy Slater, as it travelled, and closer to my winger. Jason had a bit of work to do to get past Lote Tuqiri but he did, scoring the try. Then as quick as it could set up a try, my right boot let me down. That conversion attempt was probably one of the cleanest strikes I have ever produced. But it hit the upright — flush — and almost bounced back to me.

I turned around and I could see all the boys' heads drop. I knew I had to do something to make up for it, something to win the game. It was either the whole of New Zealand hating me or loving me.

That's probably the very reason I did what I did. If I put that kick through the posts, we would have been playing for the draw, or a field goal. I didn't have any other option than to attempt to win the game with a try.

We received the ball with 77 minutes and 23 seconds on the clock, if I recall correctly, on our own tryline. The first tackle, we might have made five metres through Jason Nightingale, the second we got to the 10-metre line through Lance Hohaia. Third tackle; Jeremy Smith hit it up. Fourth; we shifted it left and made it to the 20 through Sika Manu. Fifth: Simon Mannering hit it straight up the middle of the field.

So it was the last tackle. Through the whole set, I was thinking: 'How can I win this game?' I received the ball from dummy half on the right side, and I thought the Aussies would be expecting me to chip and chase. The Australian winger Lote Tuqiri, my Tigers teammate, was back and slightly infield, where I would have been chipping to. I had played on the left side with Lote, and I knew that sometimes he would stand too flat and turn his body inwards. I saw that.

Tim must have sent a message out to watch for the chip-kick, because their fullback Billy Slater was up a bit, too. Centre Willie Tonga was infield a bit, and the forwards in the middle, who were in front of me, had just stopped.

It all felt like it was happening in slow motion. I pretended to kick, put the ball down as if I was going to, and as I did, out of the corner of my right eye I noticed that Tonga had started to come further infield, leaving my centre Shaun Kenny-Dowall outside him. Lote, meanwhile, was way back and coming in. Slater started coming forward. I thought, 'I'm not going to kick now.'

So I turned and started to take off to run. Tonga stopped his run and started to back up, but I'd beaten one of the defenders, which left him covering Bronson Harrison and Shaun, both outside me. So I threw a cut-out ball to Shaun, which I still regard as one of the best passes I've ever thrown. Shaun ran down the sideline. He could have dummied, but he sent it to Jason Nightingale. He fended off Lote. Meanwhile, I was chasing infield yelling 'Kick it, kick it', but Jason threw the ball like he'd taken the pin out of a grenade. Darren Lockyer couldn't take it; the ball bounced perfectly off his hands into mine. Brett Morris had come from the Australian right wing to try to cover it off, but I stepped off my right foot and beat him.

I honestly thought I was going to score, but at the last second, the Australian halfback Cooper Cronk had come from nowhere to tackle me. It was a huge effort from him to get there. Lance had loomed up next to me, and as Cooper got me I thought if I passed to Lance the ball might travel forward. Out of the corner of my left eye I saw Nathan Fien about 15 metres back. It was Lance or him. Because my momentum had been stopped, Lance was starting to get in front of me, so I hurled the ball over my shoulder, trying to give it some height. The ball bounced, and Fieny picked it up and scored. We had no right to come from where we did to score that try, but it was like it was just supposed to happen.

I said to the boys after the game: 'We never gave up. We could have easily thrown in the towel, but we didn't. That says something about this team.'

It was my first series win as a captain, so the victory meant a great deal to me. After being slugged by the Australians a week earlier in Auckland, no one had given us a chance. But at Suncorp, just as we did in the World Cup final two years earlier at the same ground, we did.

I felt déjà vu. We arrived back at the hotel to find our families and friends waiting for us. We didn't even go back to our rooms; we just dumped our bags downstairs. Steve wanted us to get together and talk about what had happened. We sat on chairs in a big circle, with beers in the middle, just the team and staff. A few of us cried as we spoke about what it meant to us, and what we learnt. It was some achievement. Touring is always a significant sacrifice; you're away from your families for five weeks, living out of a suitcase. But it was all worth it.

Chapter 14

A No-brainer

I ALWAYS felt like I was the smallest growing up. Until I was about 10 or 11, I was invariably the small kid who was picked last for sports at school. I was the smallest, the skinniest and the slowest. As such, there was no other way to beat the bigger players but to step them. That was the only way I felt like I could survive against them. I couldn't run around them because I was too slow; I wasn't able to run quickly until I was about 16, when I started to develop more, my legs becoming bigger and stronger.

So in the early days, I began making up, then practising, all these outrageous steps. Looking back now, they must have looked terrible, but they taught me footwork. When I was younger, just about everyone in New Zealand — or at least it felt that way — had different steps and different styles on the football field. One of them was Remus Gentles, from Auckland, who used to play for a touch football team called Galaxy. Back when I watched him play he was fairly young, but he had probably the best step of all time.

Before I had reached any sort of great heights on the touch football field, I used to watch him play. An annual touch football tournament used to be held in Whakatane in January. It was the biggest one in New Zealand, and competitors used to come from Auckland and Christchurch to play in it. The Galaxy team also included Peter Walters, a legendary touch football figure. I followed that team around to watch Remus and Peter play. As kids, we used to practise all the steps. He had so many of them.

I used to run down the street in Whakatane, stepping the cracks in the road and on the footpath. *Step on a crack; you'll marry a rat.* That was a saying back then. I'd step leaves. I'd step old ladies. I'd sidestep my brothers when they were babies. Later on, when they were older, I'd tell them: 'You can't catch me.' They'd be chasing me and I'd step them, so I could get used to having defenders come at me. I used to make them do it for hours. Mum used to love it because, exhausted, we'd come inside and go straight to sleep.

The town would be packed with people on weekends, and I'd be zigzagging through them: *step, step, step.* I used to love it. Having the coolest step could give you bragging rights back then. My signature? Jump in the air, cross the leg over, give it a bit of a wiggle, move the head a little, and when you hit the ground go bang, making a sound effect as you did it.

Bang.

Boom.

It hardly mattered how many tries you scored; it was how many people you stepped. I used to go a bit silly — I'd step someone, then I'd be about to score but I'd pull out just so I could step someone again.

When I was younger, I could only step off my right foot. That changed when I got to Keebra Park, and teams realised that I could only step off my right. I got sick of that so I started practising with my left foot. After school, I'd go home, put a pole in the backyard, or a cone, and practise stepping it. Then I would get people to run towards me, guys like Sam Moa and Joe

Action Photographics

Left: Young and testless, but not for long; official photo before my first match for the Kiwis, against Australia in April 2005.

Below: The team shot. I'm in the back row, far left. To my left are my good mates Bronson Harrison and Paul Whatuira.

Action Photographics

Action Photographics

A year later, running the ball against the Aussies in Brisbane, May 2006.

Mid-haka before the World Cup final, 22 November 2008. The Australians had advanced on us and, as you can see, I was fired up.

Job done; after the final try in the final.

The passion and the glory; our post-World Cup haka (top), and celebrating with the team (bottom).

Action Photographics

In the Four Nations of 2009 at The Stoop, Twickenham, against the Australians.

Action Photographics

The Four Nations final, against Australia, at Suncorp Stadium, 13 November 2010.

Holding the Four Nations trophy, after beating the Aussies. It was my first tournament victory as captain of the Kiwis.

Action Photographics

Action Photographics

With the man who made it happen, Kiwis coach Stephen Kearney.

Harris — after a while I got them to try to touch me, then after another while tackle me. Every day, after school, I'd be in the backyard practising the step. Now, my left-foot step has turned into my dominant step, because I practised so much.

When I started in first grade, I was only about 76 kg. When you're light, you're lighter on your feet. But that has changed over the years. I stopped practising after a while, because I was stepping too much. There was a stage when I would get the ball and step, no matter what the situation. I needed to curb it. I thought if I didn't practise it I'd stop doing it, and I was right. I can still step if I want to, but I don't need to as much. Now I concentrate on ball-playing and control.

SOME PEOPLE, though, still seem to think that I'm a one-trick pony. Or maybe two. A step and the flick. On the contrary, I'd like to think one of my best tricks is something a little less obvious. Most people think what I do is all instinct, but most of it is planned. I'm sure some people think that I don't know what I'm doing sometimes. It's rubbish. Maybe my best trick is that deception.

I analyse everything that happens in my game. If I try something, and it doesn't come off, I want to know why. Even the fancy stuff is practised and a lot of the time planned. There is not a thing I do on the field that I have not practised before on the training paddock. Tim has always said to all of us at the Tigers: 'If you're going to do something on the field, make sure you practise it at training.' Some of the second-rowers will practise grubbers at training, so if they do it in the game, depending on the situation, Tim would be comfortable with the play, because he had seen them practise it.

Anyone who has trained with me or played with me will know there isn't a lot that I do that I haven't done before. When I flick pass, I don't do it for the sake of it. People have often asked me about a try I set up, in 2009, against Parramatta. I flick-passed to Blake Ayshford to set up a try when many people thought just a conventional right-to-left pass would have sufficed.

I don't think it would have. I remember it clearly. Joel Reddy came out of the line, and I had to step past him. I got in behind him, and I showed the ball, threw the dummy and got past Jeff Robson. That's when Eric Grothe came at me and put both his hands out to grab me. If I had passed the ball conventionally, I believe he would have knocked the ball down. If I passed behind my back, he was no chance. Which is exactly what I did.

I have completed that pass a thousand times at training, so it wasn't a big deal for me. Blake knew it was coming. Because not many players do it, some people just think I do it off the top of my head. I practise flick passes every day. I am confident that I could flick pass 30 metres and hit a target. Easily. That's how much I practise. I aim at players, I aim at posts.

In the warm-ups, or after training, I'll throw them. I'll practise chip kicking. But people still think I do it all off the top of my head.

Sometimes, though, I don't feel I am given enough credit for the stuff that is not so flashy. To me, a solid game is being able to control the team to win the game. Sometimes, I feel that if I don't score a few tries and set up a few more, some feel I have not contributed. Even my family and friends are guilty of thinking like that. My mates will say to me: 'You were a bit quiet today.' I'll reply, 'Define quiet.' 'Well, you didn't do much.' 'What do you mean? I didn't miss any tackles, I kicked to the corners and chased well. I got three repeat sets.'

A NO-BRAINER

There are times when I have to step out of a game; just watch for a minute. Playmakers can't be in the game for the entire 80 minutes. Sometimes I will stand out of a set. I'll say to Robert Lui, the halfback: 'You take it.' I'll just stand back and watch the whole set. I don't watch the ball; I watch the defensive line, to see what they're doing and where I can target. Tim tells me to do it. 'Sometimes, just pull yourself out of the game,' he'd say.

It is a battle trying to find the balance in my game. I can't be too quiet, but I can't overplay my hand. If I do too much, people will say I'm trying too hard and if I don't, they will say I'm too quiet.

Still, can you actually try too hard? I don't believe that is possible. It's the way I've been brought up, the way I play. It's certainly better than not trying enough. I will never die wondering.

I OFTEN think my brain is like a calculator. It's fast at calculating what is happening. I've been trained to do something in particular situations, but my brain analyses different scenarios. If it's the last tackle, and I am setting to kick to the corner, I look at these things: where the fullback is, where the winger is, and where the space is; who is trying to put pressure on me, where they are coming from, and how hard they are chasing; and, finally, is there an opportunity to run the ball? In that order. In a split-second. That's why you will see me run the ball quite often on the last tackle, because I'm thinking: 'That winger's back deep, Blake Ayshford's outside his centre, I'll hit him.'

I always have five or six different options. I can drop the first person under me, or the second player. I can hit a lead runner or send it out the back. I could kick. I believe that is why I make a few errors sometimes; maybe I've got too many options in my head.

My role doesn't just involve knowing what I can do either. I need to know what my teammates can do. I have to adapt to who I am playing with. Playing with Blake Ayshford at left centre is different to playing with Chris Lawrence in the same position. I know what the strengths and weaknesses of my teammates are, and I know how I need to get them the ball.

The other side of that is I get the accolades for putting someone through a hole or over for a try, but they should get credit for running that line. They know where I want them to run and I know where they want to be.

I have always had good vision. Thus I don't just see who is in front of me. I can see what the players defending outside me are doing. And I do my homework. Before a game, I know that St George Illawarra's left side is up and in — in your face before you know it. So I stand deeper. I don't stand deep because I feel like it. Alternatively, if a defence is drifting, I will stand flat.

And I do not regret any mistake — because I'm trying something. I am just trying to win the game. That, ultimately, is what we are all trying to do. One of my downfalls is that I think we can score whenever we have the ball. Sometimes that is a problem, but I wouldn't change it. I'm criticised for making mistakes, taking the wrong option or running across-field. But you know what? When the team needs a try, I'm going to be trying to make it happen. My role is to make things happen, to create opportunities. I feel that if I don't play, our team will have fewer opportunities. So when I am playing, I want to make them. I used to be politically correct and say I just need to do my job, do what I have to do. But I have to do more than that. I don't feel uncomfortable about saying that either. If I played in another team, maybe I wouldn't fit in. My team's just learnt to accept it. It took them a while to get used to it, but they understand it.

I CONSIDER myself a good learner. If the coach says something to me once, I will remember it. In fact, now that I have played under him for so long, I know what Tim Sheens is thinking most of the time.

At training, we would be doing a drill, going over a couple of plays. I will call to the boys, 'We're doing the addition to the play.' Then Tim would call, 'Right, we'll do the addition to the play.' Already called it, coach. I feel prepared. I know, in whatever situation we find ourselves in, what Tim will want us to do. Robbie Farah is exactly the same. We just know him so well.

A lot of the guys who play rugby league would have found themselves sitting up the back of the class during school. But it is different when it comes to football. In my position, I think I have to sit up the front. At the back, it's easier to lose focus, to drift in and out of the meeting. If you sit up the front, the coach will see you if you are falling asleep. Plus, I like sitting up the front because everyone can see that I'm taking it all seriously and taking it all in. I will be writing much of the time. I like to set an example in that regard. If the other boys see that I'm writing, they might do so, too.

Before games, in the Tigers sheds, I try to speak to most of the players, to tell them what their job is. I'd say to Keith Galloway: 'We've got a lot of injuries, you're one of our senior forwards — you don't worry about anything today except getting us going forward and bringing our line speed in defence.' I'd say to Ben

Murdoch-Masila: 'You just talk today. Just keep talking to me, and the rest will come.' Then Tim Moltzen: 'Just follow me. If we get a quick play-the-ball coming out of our half just follow me on the inside. I'll take out the marker and the A-defender.' I never used to do it. I probably started in 2008, once I felt like I was a leader in the team. When a team revolves around your direction, I need other people to know what their job is in order to make my own job easier.

I haven't learnt it all on rugby league fields. In touch football, I had to know who to pass to. If the defence was up and in, I'd throw a long ball to the winger. I've been reading the game since I was 10 years old, even if it wasn't in the traditional environment. For any kid wanting to learn about rugby league, to develop the skills to play the game, I honestly think touch football is a wonderful base. The defenders only have to touch you when you have the ball; they don't have to tackle you. So defenders are more difficult to get past. I learnt more about agility, timing, stepping and passing. And it's fast. You just have to make sure you get rid of some of the bad habits that you can pick up when you're playing touch football. Because you only have to be touched, you can pull away a bit when a defender tries to tag you. In rugby league you have to go right to the line. The defenders have to bring you down as well.

WHEN SCOTT Prince left the Tigers, at the end of 2006, I was filthy and he knew it. I was young and, when I re-signed after the '05 grand final, I thought he would do the same. I always envisaged that we'd become one of the dominant halves pairings of all time. We were so close. I fully understand now the reasons why he had to leave. Back then I didn't. Now, I

A NO-BRAINER

also understand how his leaving might actually have helped my game, in some ways.

When he was in the team, it was hard for me to control the play whenever I wanted to. That was his job, even though it was one I always craved. When he left, I was given the opportunity to mature into that player.

If Scott was still there, my role would, I guess, remain the one I played in '05. He would control the play and I would get the ball when I called for it. He took a lot of pressure off me. He was one of the main reasons why I had such a good year; I didn't have to think much, I just ran the ball all the time. But now, I want the ball all the time, not just to run with it but to ball-play. Maybe the fact that he left was a blessing in disguise. If he was still at the club, we would be a great combination, of course, but would my ball-playing game have developed to such an extent? Could I direct and dominate? Probably not, I'd say.

When Princey joined the Gold Coast Titans, he left a hole and there was always going to be some pressure on the player who eventually took the No. 7 jersey. We had a lot of young players vying for it, so eventually Tim gave me the jersey because he knew I could handle the pressure. 'I'm going to name you at seven this week,' he said. 'What?!' 'I'm going to name you at seven.' 'Nah, nah, nah, nah,' I said. I was against it at first, but he told me my role wouldn't change that greatly. I would just get my hands on the ball more — and I had to do that anyway because Princey was gone.

Externally, the switch was made out to be a significant change, with greater challenges, when really there was little difference to the way I was playing. Tim still tries to get me to wear the No. 7 jersey every year, it seems. I tell him: 'We're not going through that again.' What's the point? Robbie Farah and I will take control of the team whichever jumpers we are wearing. Robbie plays like an extra halfback.

I must say, I didn't like the jumper. When I watch footage of me playing in the No. 7 jersey, I just don't look right. Six is my number. I don't want another. I don't even like playing in the No. 7 jersey for New Zealand.

Having the jumper did make me take control of the side, and provide more direction. I grew up a bit more playing in that number. But I still need to run, and that is why I like the No. 6 jersey.

To this day, Brett Hodgson tells me to run the ball. When I was playing with him, he'd be forever in my ear. 'What are you going to do today?' he'd say. He'd make me say: 'I'm going to run the ball.' If I didn't say it, there was a good chance I wouldn't do it, and I'd be trying the fancy stuff when it wasn't on. 'What are you going to do when you first touch it?' he'd say. 'Run the ball,' I'd reply. Now, before games, he sends me text messages: 'What are you going to do today?' Mark O'Neill is the same. He'd say: 'If you don't run the ball in your first three touches, you're a dog.' In 2010, we had a wager going — if I didn't run the ball in my first three touches, I'd have to give him $20. There were five games that year when I had to pay up; a hundred bucks in total. And we lost all five of those games. When I run the ball, I play better. When I worry about setting everyone else up, I'm not as effective. My strength's my running game and that's something I've been deliberately trying to use more.

I've always been able to ball-play — I just never had to do as much of it. If you have a look at the last four years or so, I have registered a lot of try assists as well as line-break assists. I just score a few, too, more than most five-eighths.

I get into trouble when I concentrate on ball-playing, when

A NO-BRAINER

I think about the pass before I run. The moment I think about running is when the defence has to come to me — and that's when the pass opens up.

Royce Simmons always used to say to me: 'Run first, make them come to you, then you'll pass without thinking. Think run and the pass will come.' It's no fluke that I am able to set up tries or put players through holes. I use the fact that defenders have to watch me to my advantage. If they don't come to me, I run. So I make sure they have to come to me. That creates a hole.

I can still improve greatly. My kicking game has improved out of sight since I first started in the NRL — I could kick it a long way but with no direction — but it can get better. Sometimes I feel myself not getting involved enough. Some games I would have 70 touches and then others 50.

The easy way, the cop out, would be just to do a job. For a while, that's what I thought I should be doing. Bugger that. I want to win the game. I don't want to just do my job — I want to do my job and more.

Phil Gould

EVERY NOW and then God creates a special one. Benji Marshall is such a player. Marshall has been blessed with an inner toughness and drive. The way he has come back from serious shoulder injuries at such a tender age to be out there battling with the bigger guys shows he has no fear (or has learned to deal with it).

Marshall also has been gifted with a rare set of skills. He can fire spiral passes to his left and right with ridiculous ease; make a defensive line stand still before deftly putting a teammate through a narrow opening; be hit by two or three defenders but manage a one-arm offload to a support.

BENJI

He has amazing footwork — and we're not just talking a sidestep. I have seen great sidesteppers but never anything like this. He can put two or three together with either foot to leave defenders grasping at air. Sometimes he appears to hover above the ground in slow motion before deciding which foot to bring down first. To add to the defender's confusion, the foot he plants first isn't always the one he steps off. Sometimes he doesn't step at all.

But there is something else, and I don't know what to call it. It's like his brain is a high-speed computer, continually evaluating everything and everyone around him before firing off rapid messages to his body to react.

As players come into his line of sight from any direction he determines if they are friend or foe, fast or slow.

I feel like I've been writing about Benji Marshall forever. I wrote the above in August of 2005, for my Fairfax columns. I first saw him play in a schoolboy match in the Arrive Alive Cup back in 2003. He was playing for Keebra Park State High School. I was covering this competition for Channel Nine and in preparation for the match my colleague, commentator Andrew Voss, asked me if I had ever seen this kid called Benji Marshall. 'I've heard of him; but never seen him play.' I then asked innocently: 'Is he any good?' Voss laughed: 'Yeah, he's good.'

Ten minutes into the first half, the ball filters across the field until it lands in the hands of this skinny kid who is surrounded by four defenders, and he has nowhere to go. What happened next is burned in my memory forever.

This Benji character, with absolute arrogance and almost a smile on his face, moves sideways with a bit of a shimmy. As defenders approach for the kill he taunts them with a half swerve; and then BANG; it happened. His body looks like he is going left, when all of a sudden, his left foot grips the stadium turf and he produces the biggest left-foot step you can ever

A NO-BRAINER

imagine. He leaves the defenders stranded and clutching at fresh air. He then speeds 60 metres down the touchline, outsprinting all chasers, to score an unbelievable solo try. It was breathtaking.

As I watched the slow-motion replay, trying to commentate on what I had just seen, the words just blurted out before I could stop them: 'Gee that reminds me of a young Brad Fittler!' I immediately felt sick. I hate making those kinds of comparisons with emerging players. It's unfair to label them with such titles so early in their careers. This game is hard enough without some idiot commentator branding a youngster with a reputation he won't be able to live up to. But like the speeding bullet, the spoken word can never be taken back.

Up until that point in time, Brad Fittler and Greg Alexander were the two most outstanding junior talents I had ever laid eyes upon. In the coming seasons, Benji Marshall would prove that my words, although delivered in haste, were more accurate than I could ever have imagined.

HE IS something different. He is one of those gifted players who cannot be pigeon-holed. I haven't seen anyone who reacts so instinctively to an opponent's moves since Cliff Lyons.

Lyons was a great player. If they made a highlights reel of all the tries he instigated during his long career it would take you three days to watch it. He had the rare ability to go to the line with a couple of support players and wait for the defence to react to him before he would make the play. His eyes, feet and hands would move imperceptibly and the moment the defender took one of the lures, he would instinctively know how to make him pay.

Marshall is similar, only better. When he gets the ball in his hands, he starts by making initial moves with his hands and feet and perhaps his eyes dart from side to side. I suspect his facial expressions are designed to give opponents a false impression of his intentions and his intensity. All the while he is waiting to see how those opponents react.

If they are predictable in their reaction, he cuts them in two with a swerve or a lightning step. Now, surely, this is all too much for Marshall to be thinking about at one time. That's what makes it impossible to contain him every time. Marshall doesn't know what he's going to do until it's done. He won't react to the same situation the same way every time.

Marshall is such a handful because he has absolute unshakeable belief in his ability and it now appears he cannot be intimidated or discouraged ...

When the game is on the line and time is running out there are two types of footballers: those who don't want the ball in their hands and those who say, 'Give it to me because I can make something happen.' Marshall is one of the latter. With less than five minutes left and behind by a point, he said, 'Give me the ball!'

— March 2006

I have decided to dot some excerpts of my columns through this. I researched them for this exercise and I have enjoyed reading them again. They will give an idea of what I thought of him then, just as I will describe what I think of him now.

Since that first time I saw him I have followed the evolution of Benji Marshall with great interest. At times I have been lost for words. At other times I have felt his pain as he struggled with a string of major injuries and time-consuming surgeries. I have always admired his courage. Not everything I've written over the years has been glowing in praise either.

His game has always teetered somewhere between genius and the ridiculous. I have commented on both with honesty — sometimes hoping he read the words and heeded their message.

I SEE nothing solid about his game. He's unpredictable, flamboyant and instinctive. He has the ability to conjure up the brilliant and make his opposition look silly. But he doesn't provide enough of the basic things his team needs from a player in his position.

A NO-BRAINER

Shane Warne could bowl probably eight different varieties of trick deliveries: wrong'uns, flippers, top-spinners, sliders etc. But he became great because when the pressure was on and conditions didn't suit, he could bowl the same, stock-standard leg-break delivery and land it on the spot, ball after ball, over after over, hour after hour, day after day. He would wear opponents down and pressure them into errors.

I see no such stock-standard delivery from Marshall. He's full of trick shots that excite the crowd, but under pressure, these don't always hit the mark.

— April 2007

But through it all, I have to say I have never in my life witnessed a more entertaining player than Benji Marshall. I could go and watch him play every day of the week. I don't care if he wins or loses; plays well or otherwise.

I just want to watch him play.

HE IS an enigma. A mystery wrapped up in a riddle. He is a complex combination of flamboyance, talent, skill, speed and elusiveness. He's seemingly in conflict with this ongoing battle to satisfy the expectations of us normal human beings who play and support this game. Part of you wants him to settle down into the predictable ways of the reliable performer. We want him to be an obedient servant to all the basic things we understand about our game. There is a feeling of safety in conforming to society's norms.

Marshall can be ill-disciplined. He frustrates us with his errors and apparent lack of concentration. At times he can make the simple things look so difficult. He can pull a mistake from anywhere at any time. Like yesterday when he kicked out on the full from the kick-off twice.

He'll attempt the miracle pass that isn't on. He'll throw the ball to no one and watch it bounce aimlessly across the turf into opposition hands.

But as football fans we always cheer for him because we know, at any instant, he'll give us something special to remember. In truth, we want to live out there on the edge with him . . .

The great players see things we don't see, they attempt things we wouldn't think of and they do things we could never do.

When Marshall receives the ball in the normal pattern of play, he is expected to perform the normal and premeditated tasks. However, there are the special moments where the ball lands in his hands from broken play.

Nothing is planned. He looks upfield and like a computer his brain examines the possibilities. Both he and his instincts become as excited as a hyper-active dog released from his chain.

His feet start to dance. The opposition starts to panic. The crowd rises in anticipation. Step, dummy, step, dummy, step dummy, shimmy, shimmy, whoosh he's gone.

— April 2009

My favourite moment in commentary was in the 2010 Four Nations final between Australia and New Zealand; funnily enough, at Suncorp Stadium, the very ground where I had first seen him play. Australia held the lead going into the last 10 minutes of the contest; however, the Kiwis were still in contention. They still needed two tries in the closing stages to win — a monumental task. But with a player like Marshall in their team, you know anything is possible.

At this point in the telecast there is a slight pause in proceedings and I ask the producer of our TV broadcast to get me a close-up of Marshall. I said something along the lines of: 'I wonder what's going through his mind? I wonder what it's like to know that your team's chances of victory now fall squarely on your shoulders — that it will have to be you that makes it happen. What's he thinking? How is he going to get this done?'

Marshall had this look on his face. There was a hint of urgency as he eyed the game clock — but also a sense of calm. What then happened in the final minutes of this match defied belief. Benji Marshall conjures up two tries, the second of which was on the last play of the game; on rugby league's biggest stage, against the might of the Australian Kangaroos, to win New Zealand the Four Nations Trophy.

Shortly afterwards, Benji Marshall was announced as the Golden Boot award winner for season 2010. He was named the best player in the world. The evolution of Marshall was complete. Sure he will go on to play many more games. He will win some and lose some; and he will undoubtedly contribute to both. One thing for sure is that he will always entertain.

But for mine, after that night in Brisbane, he never has to prove another thing in his life. Benji Marshall is one of the greatest talents I have ever seen. He is the reason kids love rugby league. They try to imitate him. Some will try to emulate him. But there will only ever be one Benji Marshall.

WHEN WE talk about tough footballers we generally look to the big, robust, hard-hitting, hard-running types who leave a trail of destruction in their wake.

The word tough is attributed to the players with great endurance or the ability to play long periods in games week after week, year after year.

Yep, these people are tough.

But what about the man who gets knocked down, knocked out or even seriously injured time and again, yet keeps dusting himself off to get back in the race? What about those who play under heavy scrutiny and constantly deal with the weight of expectation from the public and media. Every move they make, every pass they throw, is analysed by experts in the grandstands as though rugby league was supposed to be an exact science and players should strive for robotic consistency and accuracy.

What about the players who are given every reason to throw in the towel yet continually find the courage to keep fighting for their dreams? A tough person is capable of enduring strain, hardship or severe labour. Benji Marshall is tough for all these reasons.

Let's hope the rest of his career is played without injury. Let's hope that at all times his spirit is allowed to run free. Such an approach might scare the life out of his coaches but it sure thrills the hell out of his fans.

— October 2008

Chapter 15

Boys Will Be Boys

IN EARLY 2006, I went up to Coffs Harbour to watch a touch football tournament. I was injured at the time, having fractured my cheekbone in round one. I just wanted to watch my mates play. Every year, on the last night, after the finals, the organisers always hold a function. This one was at the Plantation Hotel. I was there drinking with my mates, trying to enjoy the night.

For some reason, some people get tough around footballers. They think they can say what they like or do what they like, to try and get a rise out of me. I had been minding my own business, when a girl approached me and asked if I'd pose for a photograph. I said: 'Yeah, no worries.' The next thing I knew, a few blokes approached me. One of them said: 'So what, you're hitting on my sister.' I told him I wasn't, but as I went to turn around, out of the corner of my eye, I saw one of them ready to throw a punch. I ducked, as one of my mates tried to push me out of the way. Two of them were trying to fight me. I pushed one of them, and then the other guy started swinging at me. He got me on the side of the head. My mates, who had been behind me, stepped in front of me, as one of them just went nuts, trying to throw glasses at me.

I had no idea what was happening, and I don't think those guys did either. They seemed to be so off their heads, they wouldn't have known what they were doing. I just left straight away.

A few days later, I read about me being in a brawl. I'd done nothing really. I'd pushed a guy, trying to defend myself, and got out of the way. But it was reported that I was in a pub brawl, that I'd been knocked out. I had a lump on my head in the morning, but I wasn't knocked out. I couldn't believe it. It was at a time when I was starting to be recognised more, and I realised I had to be more wary. Drunk people would approach me and talk to me, and when I told them I'd like to talk to my mates again, they would take offence. The worst part was I knew that anyone could hit me first and knock me to the ground, but if I got up and hit them back, it would be me being the focus in the papers.

Sure enough, the following year, I was at a Bondi Junction hotel with a number of footballers. Someone got into an argument, and I attempted to cool it down. A guy pushed me, and tried to throw a punch. I moved out of the way, and Mark Riddell, who was just trying to have a beer, as we all were, tried to step in — one guy reached over with a glass and smashed it on Mark's head. Before I knew it, I was outside, wondering what just happened and how it happened.

THE YEAR after that, I was at a Kings Cross bar, the Sapphire Suite, for a friend's birthday. I wasn't even drinking on the night. There were some guys there who were hanging around us, and I was talking to them for a while.

They seemed to be okay people. I didn't mind talking to them. One of them said: 'Can I get a photo, mate?' I said: 'Yeah, sweet.' The other guy took the photo with a digital camera. Then the guy who had been in the photo with me grabbed me in a headlock. My mate said: 'You can't do that, man.' I asked him: 'What's that about?'

'What are you going to do about it?' he said. I replied: 'I don't have to do anything about it.' I was just starting to walk away, when the guy took a swing at me. I moved out of the way, and held his head down. I looked up and his mate was snapping photographs of me. Sure enough, one of the photos later appeared in the paper. The guy who took the photo had sold it.

The police were called. I told them what happened, they checked the CCTV footage and they cleared me of any wrongdoing. They kicked the bloke out. But the focus of the night became me being in a nightclub brawl. There was no brawl. I still believe to this day I was set up. You don't talk to someone in that manner for so long, and then in an instant, snap. And why was his mate ready with the camera to take the photo? He'd just taken the photo of me and he still had it in his hands, poised. The photos were auctioned off to the highest bidder.

There have been so many occasions when someone has said something to me, and I would have dearly loved to respond physically. I would have loved to put one on their chin. But I haven't. That's what a lot of them want me to do. I can deal with a lot of what people say to me, but some people cross the line.

For a time, I used my teammate Jamahl Lolesi as a minder. When he signed with the Tigers, we became really close. We have similar personalities and he lived with me for a while. He would always say to me: 'If you go out, make sure I come with you.' He had seen what it was like for me.

On more than 10 occasions, people approached me and would become angry because I would pose for a photograph with them and then want to turn around to talk to my friends again. They would try to start something, but Jamahl would step in and play the bodyguard role. There would be times he had to belt people. Someone would approach me and try to hit me, and he would step in. He used to protect me. I've had women throw drinks over me. They would want a photograph and they would want to keep talking, but all I would want is to talk to my friends. And I would wear a drink as a result. Going out, trying to enjoy a night out, can have its downside.

SOMETIMES, THEY can start off so well, too.

When your old man is dying, and he tells you he wants something, you do what you can to make it happen. So I decided to help kids with cancer. But I've got to say, the hard work was done by others. My manager, Martin, and the Children's Cancer Institute of Australia, helped enormously in setting up the Benji Marshall Foundation. All I really did was put my name to it, and say a few words on the night of the major fundraiser.

The dinner, in March 2011, was a memorable one. What happened after it won't alter my fondness for it. I wanted to honour my father and I feel I did.

The hardest part of the night, the Footy Rocks fundraiser, was standing up in front of the audience and talking about Dad; explaining why I wanted to help.

As with my eulogy, I had notes written down, but I ultimately did not use them. I find speeches like that come off better when you just speak, when there is nothing prepared. I told the people in attendance everything, about why I set up the Foundation, about what my dad had said to me on the last morning we spent together. I don't recall there being a dry eye in the house. I interviewed parents who had to speak about how their own lives, their own children, were touched by cancer. They spoke of children who had fought and lost, and children who had fought and were still fighting. As they spoke, many in tears, memories of my own were brought back. I asked questions based on my own experiences with my father's battle. It made people open their hearts, and their pockets.

When I was told that the dinner had raised almost $250,000, I was very emotional. I wondered if the old man would be proud of me. I certainly felt proud of myself. I wasn't sure what we could achieve, but I didn't think we could reach that figure.

That money would go to children's cancer research at the CCIA laboratory. All because my old man asked me to do something. I hoped to improve on that the following year, and the year after that.

I have seen many hospitals and, thus, many sick children. It is awful to think how many there are in hospitals across the city and across the state right now. I have seen parents who live in with their children, forced to quit their jobs to look after their sick or dying son or daughter. I try never to say no to a hospital visit. When it comes to sick children, I could never say no. It is something I hate seeing. But you never know. It could be me one day looking for support.

I HAD my friends and relatives with me and I was proud of the achievement. I felt relieved, too, knowing I had satisfied Dad's dying wish in getting the Foundation up and running. I wanted to celebrate it with them. We walked up the road from the Four Seasons hotel, along George Street, to the Establishment bar. I was with my mum, Lydia, and her partner, as well as Uncle Bensy, Aunty Michelle, my girlfriend Zoe, and more than a dozen of my mates.

We were there for about an hour and a half. Some of my friends and relatives had been drinking at the function, so by 3 a.m., those of us who were left were ready to finish up. On the way back, some of the girls were hungry. We walked into McDonald's to get something to eat; the girls ordered and I went straight to the corner with some of my mates to sit down.

The girls bought too much food, and I signed autographs and posed for photographs. Everything was calm.

We finished our food, but we still had about four burgers left, so we offered them to a man at the table next to us, who had only bought a small chips and small drink himself. He was over the moon; the boys shook his hand and he thanked us. He said he didn't have much money.

We all walked outside. Half of the group crossed the street on the way back to the hotel, but I stayed outside the restaurant for at least 15 minutes, signing more autographs and posing for more photographs. The longer I stayed there, the more it seemed likely that I wouldn't get away. It started to drag on; people would walk past, see me and stop. Then the next group would. Then the next. A few of my friends stayed with me to make sure everything was okay. Everyone was in good spirits, though.

People were yelling things. 'The Tigers are shit.' I heard: 'Darren Lockyer shits on you.' I hear that sort of stuff all the time. We started walking off, and waited for the lights to turn green on the corner of Bridge and George Streets. Zoe was on the other side of the road, waiting for me and two of my mates.

I started crossing the road when the lights changed. I heard something. I didn't think I could have heard properly. I turned around and said: 'What did you say?' I knew who said it. It was a bloke from the same group who had been yelling the same stuff earlier. He said the same thing: 'F*** off you black c***.' I said: 'You can't say that. If you want to say it, say it to my face.' He leant towards me, bringing his face closer in to mine, and said it again.

I said: 'I don't need this shit.' I pushed him away to get him out of my face. I didn't punch him. Everything that followed happened so quickly but it came out in evidence in court that the bloke was punched in the face by someone else almost immediately after I pushed him. I went back to the hotel, and didn't mention what happened to anyone. I had a good night's sleep. I was satisfied with the night.

Around lunchtime the next day, I received a phone call from Stephen Humphreys, the Wests Tigers chief executive. He told me someone had gone to the police and alleged that I had punched him, cutting his lip open.

My heart dropped. I thought it couldn't be right. I waited. Next thing I knew, my mobile phone was ringing constantly. It was all over the television news and on the front page of newspapers the next day.

WHAT FOLLOWED after that night was an enormously difficult period. The amount of negative publicity which so swiftly came my way, without the truth being made public, was difficult to accept. There were a lot of assumptions being made about me, which I had no control over.

On the Sunday, Stephen Humphreys and Tigers board member David Trodden said they needed to see me. They told me we would need to go to the police station and I was to effectively hand myself in.

I had been staying with Zoe, so I had to head up the road to the Zanerobe clothing warehouse (the company is owned by two friends of mine, Leith Testoni and Jonathan Yeo) at Mosman, where I picked up a suit and shirt. I bought shoes at a shop nearby. There were cameras waiting for me out the front of the police station, at North Sydney. I walked in and, after introductions, was told I was under arrest. I was read my rights. I was asked if I wished to make a statement. My legal advice was not to. I simply could not understand why I had been arrested. I did not believe I had done anything wrong. It was around the time of Mardi Gras in Sydney, so I had to wait for people who were on drugs charges. I was thinking to myself as I waited: 'I haven't sold drugs, I haven't punched anyone. What am I doing here?'

The number of cameras had swelled by the time I left. The police were kind enough to allow me to go down through the basement and out the back door. Stephen asked one of the officers to bring the car down to the basement, but he couldn't get the handbrake off! The media knew something was up so by the time we left in the car there were cameras waiting. I felt like I was a fugitive, on the run.

I had to leave my home for five days, because the media was camped out the front, out the back and even in the trees. There were camera crews trying to film over my balcony into my home. Tim Moltzen, who lives with me, told me.

I drove past in a friend's car on one occasion; there was no way I was stopping to get out. They were standing around my car, waiting for me.

At another time, I went to Martin's house, in my car, and got out to be greeted by two camera crews getting out of their cars. I jumped back into my car and made a getaway. I organised a secret meeting place where I could catch up with people; at the Zanerobe offices.

Wherever I went, I was paranoid about who was looking at me, and what they were doing there.

The media tried to follow me in their cars. On one occasion, I got to a set of traffic lights and, just as they were turning orange, I tapped the brakes and then sped up through the intersection. I got away. Then I had to go into town to see my barrister, Geoff Bellew. I went into his office. As I was leaving, he told me there was a chance there could be some cameras outside. I put my hood on, trying to hide as much as I could. Sure enough, there were the cameras.

Head down, I walked away. I wondered why no one was following me. It turned out they were filming a television show in that part of town. It had nothing to do with my own soap opera.

The media was just waiting for me to say something. I didn't want to talk to them. There was nothing, really, I could say. I drove back towards Martin's house. On the way, I telephoned him and he told me: 'Don't worry, there's no one on my street. I've had a look.' I got out of the car in his street and, just as I arrived at his front door, a couple of cameramen jumped out of their cars. I sprinted back to mine and drove off again. They tried to follow me; I lost them at a set of traffic lights again. It was just crazy.

I ended up getting back into my apartment through my garage, in someone else's car. I was lying on the back seat of my mate's car, which had tinted windows. From the street, you can look through a window directly at the lift on my floor. So I lay on the floor of the lift and, with not a word of a lie, crawled to my front door, before opening it up.

I looked out of a crack in my blinds, and there were dozens and dozens of people outside my building, waiting. 'Oh my God,' I thought. 'This is just out of control.' I turned on the television news and I was the major story of the night on every single channel. What for? For nothing. The second story was a man who was killed after being stabbed in the head at Bankstown. That put the whole experience into perspective. 'What is going on?' I thought.

To get out again, I had to ask my mate to drive into the garage, so I could lie on his back seat again. I stayed with my girlfriend for a few days.

The club wanted me to say something publicly. So I did. I arrived at the press conference, at Concord Oval, to find it was being broadcast live by some channels. As the media were waiting in their cars at the entrance to the ground, I snuck in over the other side of the stadium in Tim's car. Hiding away again I felt like I was in some sort of real-life hide-and-seek.

The press conference was so overwhelming. There were so many eyes on me. I read out a statement, but I could not answer any questions because anything else I said might jeopardise my defence. It was frustrating in a way. There was a lot being said and written about me that was not true, and I could not reply. I could not set things straight. I could not clear my name, which was being muddied. Still, the more information that came out, the more things appeared to be turning my way. I did have people on my side. I stood there signing so many autographs on the night of the fundraiser. It, unfortunately, led to something else, and I found myself drowning in negativity.

I have tried to forget the whole experience. The only way I thought I could respond was to play well on the field. But that was difficult because I was going through so much turmoil off it. It was difficult to focus on football.

It was the hardest period of my life. I put on a brave face to convince people that it wasn't bothering me, but every time

I went home, I would be thinking about what was going to happen to me, and how people were perceiving me. I had so much support, though. Stephen Humphreys and David Trodden were wonderful support for me, as was Tim Sheens and my teammates. Ditto my family, my girlfriend Zoe. If I didn't have that support, I would have gone insane. It's not an easy thing to deal with, not being able to go home, because cameras are in trees outside your home. I feel like I am strong enough to handle most things, but at times, I felt sick.

IT WAS the longest five months of my life, but eventually I would have my day in court. It was one of the scariest things I have ever done.

I had never been in a courtroom before. I hadn't been near one. So I had no idea what to expect.

My case was due to commence at 9.30 a.m. I arrived about 8.15, not wanting to be late. It worked for me in a way, because there were only a few cameras waiting for me when I arrived at the Downing Centre Local Court.

I had to put on a confident front, a brave face. When I get scared or nervous, I always seem to laugh. That's my 'tell'. It's my way of trying to show that I'm not struggling. But inside, I was churning.

I went upstairs and sat in a room. I waited and waited. The start was eventually delayed because the CCTV footage couldn't be played on the computer. It eventually began about 11 a.m.

As I was waiting to go into the courtroom, people were asking me for autographs and photos. I could not believe it. A lady, the chaplain of the court, told me if there was anything she could do for me, she would do it. 'A few prayers would be nice,' I replied.

When I walked inside the courtroom, there was no room for all the people who came to support me. They were all taken up by reporters. We had to find extra seats for Stephen, David and Martin. It was all quite overwhelming. The only courtroom I had seen was on television, on *Law and Order*.

I was drained after the first day. And listening to these blokes who were accusing me, I found it difficult to bite my tongue. I knew I was innocent, but with all the evidence that the other blokes were giving, denying that the bloke had made a racist taunt against me . . . I was scared.

I took the stand on the second day. As I waited, my hands were shaking. And my hands never shake. They are usually so steady, but I was looking down at them and I could not stop them. I had to put one hand on the other and press them both on the table in front of me.

When I was called, I was more nervous than I had been before any game I have played. I felt exhausted, too. Once it all started, I felt much better. I felt a lot like I did before I gave Dad's eulogy. I was in knots before but I was given strength once I had started. Mum reckoned Dad was looking after me from above. It was his birthday a few days after.

The prosecutor seemed like he was trying to put words in my mouth. I kept saying to him: 'No, those are your words, they're not my words. I never said that.' Then he started asking me about rugby league. He asked me if I did boxing training, and if I went out onto the field to hurt people. I don't go out there to hurt people; I do so because I love playing the game. I make the tackles because I don't want to let any of my mates down. It's not a sport where we practise to hurt people. I hate seeing people get hurt in rugby league.

'Well, what's your job?' he asked me. I was thinking to myself:

'Is this bloke serious? Where are we going with this?' I said: 'Make the outside backs look good.' There were a few giggles; it helped me relax a bit.

I felt like I was hearing the same questions over and over, and I was giving the same answers.

The hardest part of the whole two days was hearing the final submissions. Hearing the prosecutor put doubt in my own mind, so I started to think to myself: 'Am I in trouble here?' But then when my barrister, Geoff Bellew SC, gave his submission, I was comforted.

The Magistrate left the room to make her decision. After she returned, the longer she spoke, the more I felt I was going to be okay. Then I heard: 'Case dismissed.' I sat there. All the people behind me were moving out of the courtroom. The reporters ran out. I still sat there. I didn't know what I was supposed to do. I didn't know if it was finished or not. So I sat there.

My barrister, Geoff, and solicitor, John Byrnes, turned around and said: 'Congratulations.' They turned again towards the Magistrate. So I sat there.

'You can get up,' one of them said. I breathed the biggest sigh of relief. I felt as if a 10 kg weight immediately lifted off my shoulders. I phoned some of my relatives. They already knew, the news having spread fast. It was five months of stress, of worry. Worrying what people were thinking of me. That is something I don't usually do. It was a difficult time for my family; they were constantly defending me in public.

Trying to focus on football was enormously difficult. I pretended that everything was okay, but I'm a human being. Anyone out in that position would feel uncomfortable. It was the hardest thing I have ever had to go through.

I will make this point, though. In spite of it all, I never, ever, felt like I had somehow failed in honouring my late father, because of what happened on that night. That never crossed my mind. He would have been proud of everything I did that night. Everything. If he was here today, he would have told me that. That, I am sure of.

Everyone at the function had seen how important the night was to me. I didn't have a drink at the dinner because I was so focused on the fundraiser being a success. I went from being so happy and emotional to being a different kind of emotional. It was awful to think that the fundraising dinner might have been overshadowed by what happened later. It felt awful knowing that many people were reporting on it and not mentioning why I found myself in the position I did, that I had been at a charity function. The fact that I was out late at night in the city suddenly became an issue. If I cannot go to McDonald's in the city, down the road from the hotel I was staying at, to get something to eat after a function like that, there is a real problem somewhere. Is it a rule for footballers that they should never be out after three o'clock in the morning?

Why? Oh, that's right. Because we're not normal people. How are we meant to be normal when there is a different set of rules for us?

It made me not want to go out, that's for sure. Not going out is the only way to ensure, for certain, that there is no trouble. What else can I do?

Chapter 16

The Next Step

ALLOW ME if you could, an opportunity to reflect a little. I had always planned to go on a holiday after the World Cup in 2008 with a few of my touch football mates. I played with them in the State Cup touch football tournament, won that, then Jamie Stowe and Adam Lollback and I had a trip around the USA and Canada. We flew into Los Angeles, spent a few nights there, then moved to San Diego, which is one of the most beautiful cities I've seen. We knew we had an early-morning flight to Las Vegas, so we went straight from the nightclub back to the hotel, to pick up our bags and our snowboards, and went to the airport in the same transporter taxi. The first thing I saw after disembarking the plane in Vegas was a poker machine; the old-style variety with the pull-down arm. It was still 7 a.m., but it felt like night-time, with all the bright lights of the advertising. We hired a Hummer to take us to our hotel, the MGM Grand.

We got out, with our snowboards, and people must have been looking at us thinking: 'Who are these people?' Funnily enough, two Australians walked in about the same time and recognised me. They asked me for a photograph. I could see the porter and the people at reception looking at me. One of the Aussies told the people at reception that I played football in Australia. When

I got to the front desk, one of them said: 'Are you guys famous?' My mates said: 'Yeah, he's famous.' They actually Googled me. The manager came down and upgraded us to a celebrity suite! We were there for seven nights in a celebrity suite straight out of *The Hangover*. We felt like kings.

We walked into the room about 8.30 a.m. to complimentary champagne and bottles of vodka. We went out to a few clubs. I was just so relaxed; no one knew me, I didn't feel any pressure to behave in a certain way. I could really let my hair down and enjoy myself. At one stage I fell off my stool as I leaned over to get my drink; instead of kicking me out, the bouncer picked me up, sat me back on the stool, put the bourbon back in my hand and made me sip it. 'I love Vegas,' I thought. We took some people we'd just met back to our suite to have a little party about 4 a.m.

I was sick halfway through the week. Not because of alcohol consumption but because of the buffet. I suffered food poisoning, and the hotel had to call the house doctor. I had to sit in my room for two nights while the boys went out and partied. I watched 11 episodes of *CSI: Miami* in my room. I eventually came around and we went to a David Copperfield show. Stowie got called up on stage. A few days later we read in the paper that one of Copperfield's tricks had gone horribly wrong, and one of his assistants was sucked into a fan, having his face cut and his arm broken. Stowie felt a little sick. While we were in Vegas it snowed for the first time in about 30 years.

We flew to Reno, caught the bus to Salt Lake City and then Lake Tahoe. I'd never seen countryside as beautiful. The snow was like white powder. We had a ball snowboarding, although Adam hurt his knee.

We made our way to San Francisco en route to Vancouver.

THE NEXT STEP

We stopped over in Seattle, where it was snowing heavily. We landed on the slippery runway, but then couldn't take off again. Seattle Airport was closed down, and we were forced to wait about 10 hours to find our bags. The airport was chaotic. We proceeded to book out a limousine, replete with chains on the tyres, which took us to our hotel near the Seattle Tower. We had no concrete plans so we stayed there for a couple of days. We met some people who were in the same situation as we were, snowed in. We drank vodka, ate Spam, made snow angels in our undies and, would you believe, watched *Sleepless in Seattle*.

WITH THE airport still closed, we made other arrangements. We eventually purchased the last three tickets for a ferry leaving from Seattle to Vancouver. We needed to be at the dock at 5 a.m. We saw some whales during the eight-hour trip, so it was certainly a more picturesque way to travel than by plane. We caught a bus from Vancouver to Whistler. There, we met a Ski-doo instructor, who took night tours. We had to do tests to make sure we were competent on the Ski-doos. He took us on tracks which were just about untouched, with fresh powder up to your waist. We reached a track which looked like a big field, and he told us we could go as fast as we wanted. The guide told us to drive in a figure eight. I stayed with him, trying to keep up. Stowie and Adam were behind me. The guide put his hand in the air, motioning me to stop. There were two snowmobiles which had flipped over an edge into a deep pile of snow. He said: 'We need to help.' I turned around to tell Stowie and Adam what had happened, but they weren't there. It was them in the pile of snow. They were buried up to their necks and we had to dig them out.

Canada was beautiful. We had an amazing time over there and it did me the world of good. Why am I telling you all this? It also showed me what life would be like if no one knew me again, bar the hotel lobby in Vegas, and the celebrity suite. I can't go to a supermarket without being stopped. I feel like I have to wear a hood and a hat wherever I go. I sometimes don't feel like I have my own life to live any more. I am constantly wrestling with the dilemma of having to act normal when I don't feel normal. And I can't handle it sometimes. Footballers are told they cannot do what people their own age are doing, but yet they need to act normal. What's normal? The scrutiny has reached another level. Sometimes, I wish that I didn't live in Sydney. I get recognised in Melbourne now. AFL people will approach me and say: 'You're the guy who got in a fight.'

FOLLOWING THE scrutiny that came with that night, I thought to myself: 'I'm ready to stop playing.' If that was what it was going to take for me not to have to deal with the scrutiny, that was what I thought I would have to do. If that was what it was going to take for me to feel normal again . . .

I feel conscious of people looking at me. They are. I've gotten over it now, but there was a stage when I would look at people, and I would see their lips move — *That's Benji Marshall* — and it really annoyed me.

Sometimes, I just wish that I could have a normal life. It's probably selfish and unfair of me, but sometimes I wish I didn't play rugby league. I wish I'd done something else. I wish I'd been successful at something that didn't require me to be under pressure all the time. That's what it feels like to me. A constant pressure to be on my best behaviour. Like I'm at boarding school and I'm being threatened with the strap. I feel caged sometimes. I don't wish to end this on a negative thought. But it is the truth. It is how I have felt and it is how I feel.

Imagine working in an office, where everyone watched what you do all day. All eyes on you for a day, a week, a month.

Some of my friends wonder why I don't want to go out to have dinner. My girlfriend didn't understand for a while. My life is under a microscope. It feels like I am constantly being watched, like there is a satellite camera on me. Again, I am probably being selfish, but has it been worth it? Has it been worth the pressure? Has it been worth sacrificing a normal family life? I don't get enough time to spend with my family, and the time I do get, it's difficult to put to good use. I feel like I've neglected some of my family. I can't be the person they want me to be. Some of them may be let down by me, by the fact that I can't spend the time with them that I ought to. I feel terrible that I haven't kept in touch with some of my family. Some, I might see only once a year. We used to be so close and I feel like I've pushed some of them away from me. My brothers — I feel awful for them. When they moved over here, they always heard: 'You're Benji's brother.' Look what they've got to live up to. I try to tell them, 'Be yourself,' and 'Do whatever you want to do.' Their life is going to be under the spotlight. And it's because of me. It's my fault. Jordan has trouble dealing with it. In an interview, he said: 'I just want to be me.' I can understand where he's coming from.

I had always wanted him to look up to me, and be like me. But he's seen what it is like for me. He doesn't want to be that; he just wants to be himself.

My brothers won't tell me what they're thinking because they're somehow embarrassed to. They don't want to disappoint me. But they forget that I helped raise them. I know what they're feeling. It's got to the point where they feel like they cannot confide in me the way they used to.

I had always wanted to provide for my brothers. I wanted them to have what I didn't. That was one of my main motivations for being successful. I give them money every week; I'll hand Jeremy a $50 allowance. But I don't like the fact that they are in my shadow.

The worst part about this game is that it has made me go into my shell, and make me just want to be by myself. I will get home from training and I will not want to see anyone. I won't want anyone to see me. At home, by myself, is the only time I don't feel pressure. I know I can trust myself.

If I go to a pub, I've got to scan the room to see who's drunk, who could be dangerous to me later. 'Okay, this guy's getting a bit carried away, coming at me, I'd better leave.' These are all things that not everyone can appreciate. Who's the bad guy in the room? I have to look around, and sit in a corner behind all my mates, to make sure there's no trouble. If somebody hits me, and I hit them back, it will make the papers. We are taught to be competitive, and in a game, if someone hits you, you hit them back. Off the field, if someone punches you in the head, what do you do? You have to just walk away. We're taught to stand up for ourselves, against bullying, yet we can't.

If I want to have a drink by myself, not talk about football, and not be bothered, I go to my local pub. It is where I seek solace and solitude. I know all the locals and all the bar staff. I can sit in my corner. That pub is the reason I live where I do.

There have been times I have sat in my room and cried about all this. Not just once or twice, but a dozen times. What can I do? There is nothing I can do. How can I live a normal life? I'm expected to do just that, by everyone: the media, the NRL, the

THE NEXT STEP

fans. What life do I have? Football players don't get the chance to have a life away from the sport. If they do, it's frowned upon. What is normal? I ask myself that every day.

Then there is the criticism. After we were beaten well by South Sydney at the Sydney Cricket Ground in 2010, a couple of kids, maybe eight or nine years old, took their Wests Tigers jerseys off as I was walking off the field and threw them at me. 'What's this?' I said. 'You can have the jersey,' one of them said. 'We don't go for Wests Tigers any more.' Then they ran back to their parents, who were laughing. That was difficult to take, having kids who look up to you do that. I just dropped the jerseys on the ground and kept walking. It's not like we go out and lose by 50 points on purpose. It's not like we enjoy doing it.

SOMETIMES, I have felt that I am lost, that I'm not sure of my purpose. All I want to do is play rugby league. All the stuff that comes with it is not enjoyable, so why am I playing? There have been three or four occasions when I've considered giving the game away as a result. Everything was going quite well at the time, but I just knew I had no life. I couldn't just hang out with my family. The doubts came after my trip away to the USA. It opened my eyes again to what life would be like when I could just hang out with my mates and not feel the pressure.

Thinking back to that nightclub in Las Vegas, I wonder what would happen if I fell off a bar stool in Sydney. For a good month or so afterwards, I wanted the life that I had experienced ever so briefly again. I could do anything and no one would care. I could have pinched something from a shop, and the only people who would have cared would have been Uncle Phil or my mum, who would have given me a hiding. I wanted that life again.

THE SCRUTINY is intense and the rumours are regularly incorrect. There always seems to be speculation that Robbie Farah and I do not get on and that we clash. We came through the squad at about the same time. I can honestly say that there has never been anyone at the Tigers that I haven't gotten along with.

I've been and stayed good friends with most of the players I've come across. Those rumours get to me. We all have our moments. Robbie is the type of person who won't talk to anyone if Liverpool loses. But we are good mates, and I'm close with all my teammates. It's difficult to say this categorically, not having played with any other club, but I really believe there could not be a closer group of players in the competition than the Tigers.

That said, there is not one player in our team I haven't had a blow-up with. That just comes with the territory. In my position, if things don't get done, I need to say something. Because I feel like a leader in the team, I do it. I've had arguments with Tim, Robbie, Chris Heighington, Brett Hodgson . . . everyone. I've had blow-ups with the coach. I am happy to cop a spray from the coach, because it makes me train harder. I like it. That's his job; he's the coach. If he didn't tell me what to do, he wouldn't be doing his job. Just because we have a good relationship, it doesn't mean we don't clash from time to time. But if we have an argument at training, it doesn't bleed into our relationship off the field. If I believe something is right, I will argue it, either until he believes me or he convinces me otherwise. You need a coach who can tell you: 'That's not good enough.' If you're not told, maybe you won't see it.

In '06, I was having a bad week, and the senior guys were coming down hard on me. I said to Hodgo, 'I'm sick of you old blokes telling me what to do.' I might have used the word 'blokes', I might not have. I was out of line and he lost it. I was frustrated and I felt like they were all picking on me.

The older guys gave it to me for weeks. It just happens. Rugby league is a contact sport. Teammates can get into physical altercations at training. Then afterwards, you're hugging about it.

That's the nature of the beast. There is so much testosterone involved, and everyone is being physical. Of course, someone isn't going to like it if they get hit in the head. They have been taught to react to that from day one.

People hear about it, though, and think that it's personal.

Sometimes, really personal. I do not know how the rumour emerged this year about me sleeping with Liam Fulton's wife, and that Bryce Gibbs and I had had a fight, but it was disgraceful. We first heard about it when Keith Galloway said to us at training: 'My brother's just rung me and asked if there was a fight at training between Bryce and Benji.' Keith told him there hadn't been. 'Well, apparently, Benji's been having an affair with Liam's wife, Bryce took offence to it and bashed him at training,' his brother said. We all thought it was a joke. We were laughing about it. There were people who were claiming: 'I was there, I saw the fight.' There was no fight at training. Next thing I knew, there was a vague story about it on the news; that there had been a scuffle at training. I phoned Liam and said: 'What's going on?' It began to spiral out of control.

The whole team was put on a conference call. We could not believe it was happening. Then the rumours kept escalating. We were getting more phone calls about it. It just went viral and it went international. I had people from the Gold Coast phoning me, and even people from overseas asking me about it.

The worst part was, people were actually saying to me:

'Is it true?' I got pretty cranky at a lot of my mates for asking me that question. Anyone who knows me should realise I would never do that.

The irony was, with Bryce and Liam's futures at the club up in the air at the time, I was fighting for them, backing them up. Bryce made his debut just after mine; we had all come through around the same time. It just poured petrol on the fire, making life as I know it so difficult. There always seem to be people wanting to bring you down. But there were other people who were impacted in this case. Our families were dragged into it.

I explained it to my girlfriend. I have always been very loyal to all my friends. I would never do something like that. I sat down with Liam at one stage. He actually said he felt sorry for me.

FUNNILY ENOUGH, the one thing that stopped me from quitting was my teammates. I didn't want to let them down. I still don't. I know I am playing for them, but I don't feel like I am playing for myself. I'm playing to give my family a good life, but what's it giving me? I don't feel like my life is, well, fun. I still get the same thoughts on occasions, about giving it away. I know I won't, because I don't want to let anyone down. I feel like I'm strong enough to get through those hard times, but I just feel like if it keeps building up . . . I'm going to explode. It's a constant in my head, pumping and pumping.

Sometimes, in games, I will be frustrated, and I will make rash decisions. Tim will see it and ask, 'What's wrong?' I can't explain it to him, why I am so frustrated. I can't explain it to anyone else. The moment you show vulnerability, people will take advantage. My family looks up to me. I am strong, but I'm human too. There

THE NEXT STEP

are things that hurt me as well. I'm not superhuman.

I feel like I should be normal, but I don't feel normal. I don't feel famous, and I don't prance around thinking I'm famous. What am I? Who am I? That, not even I can answer. People say: 'I'd love your life, it's so easy.' I'm here to say it's not. I would love anybody to swap shoes with me for a week, and maybe understand what it is like, to be under pressure every day. I do not wish for any sympathy; this is no cry for help. Don't get me wrong. I am fortunate, and I'm grateful for the talent I was given. But talent only goes so far. It's the hard work that takes you further. And it is hard work.

I know there will be people who will criticise me for saying all this. My purpose for doing so? I am simply trying to explain what it is like to be me. I am trying to explain what I feel. That is the point of this, surely. People are entitled to their opinion and they can criticise me for being honest. What I am trying to say is that my life is not the glitz and glamour that many would think. Mine is not the easiest life.

I am blessed, certainly. I get paid to do something I love doing. And I get paid well. But I will be paid that much for a limited time. For what? To ruin my body? To have four shoulder reconstructions? To require a shoulder replacement by the time I'm 40 years old? We, footballers, are destroying our bodies. Head knocks, concussions . . . if people wish to criticise, they can. But until someone lives it, they cannot understand.

I just yearn for the time when people can. Not having a father never bothered me, because I had so many. But I have been through so many life experiences . . . I always thought I could write a book.

Would I have taken a different path had I known what I know now? Sometimes I think that I would have. If I could just play football, I would take that. If I'd known that I wouldn't have a know me, they have a totally different opinion of me. People think they know me because of the person they see on *The Footy Show* or the me they see on the field. They might think I am cocky, that I am arrogant. But if I don't act that way when I play, I can't do what I do. When I get off the field, there's no need for me to act that way.

I'm quite relaxed, really. The way I play, and the attitude I have on the field, is the direct opposite of my attitude off the field.

I still feel like I've been given this life to help people, and to influence people's lives; to help children with cancer or simply inspire some kids. Until people get to know me, they won't know me.

For the people who have pigeon-holed me in a certain way — they can think that. I know that I probably look that way on the TV. But my life's not about being a football star, earning X amount of dollars and being better than anyone. I feel like my life is about putting a smile on Lleyton's face, helping other kids, helping my friends and family financially. I feel like I've been given a job to do.

It only started to make sense after my father passed away. Before that, my purpose never really made any sense. It has taken a while. Better late than never, I guess. If any of my friends come to me needing help, I will help them, whether they need a place to stay or a bit of money.

Whether I like it or not . . . whether I like what comes with it or not . . . I don't have a choice. I can complain about it as much as I want. And, yes, sometimes it sucks. But according to Lleyton's father, my team has added months or maybe even years to his life. How can you beat that? You have to be in the hospital to understand how you have put a smile on the face of someone who has cancer. That has an effect on you. It makes me proud.

There are things I find hard to understand about myself. Why do I get so upset about the lifestyle that I have when it is a good one? It is hard for me to comprehend why. I get frustrated all the time with myself for doing so. Sometimes, I have tantrums to myself about what I have to put up with. I probably contradict myself for saying all this. I am doing the very thing that frustrates me: complaining about my life and what comes with it.

I feel like I have found my purpose in life . . . but at a cost. That said, it's a price I'm willing to pay. If I look back and think of all the people I have helped, it *has* been worth it in the end.

About the Writer

As a reporter for *Rugby League Week* and then the *Sydney Morning Herald*, Glenn Jackson has covered 13 NRL grand finals. One of his highlights was the 2005 decider, which saw Benji Marshall and his Wests Tigers side come of age against North Queensland. After seven years with *RLW*, covering the 2000 rugby league World Cup in England, Glenn joined the *Herald* in 2006. In his time there he has covered Marshall's World Cup win in 2008 and the Four Nations triumph of 2010, as well as the bumps in his career in between.

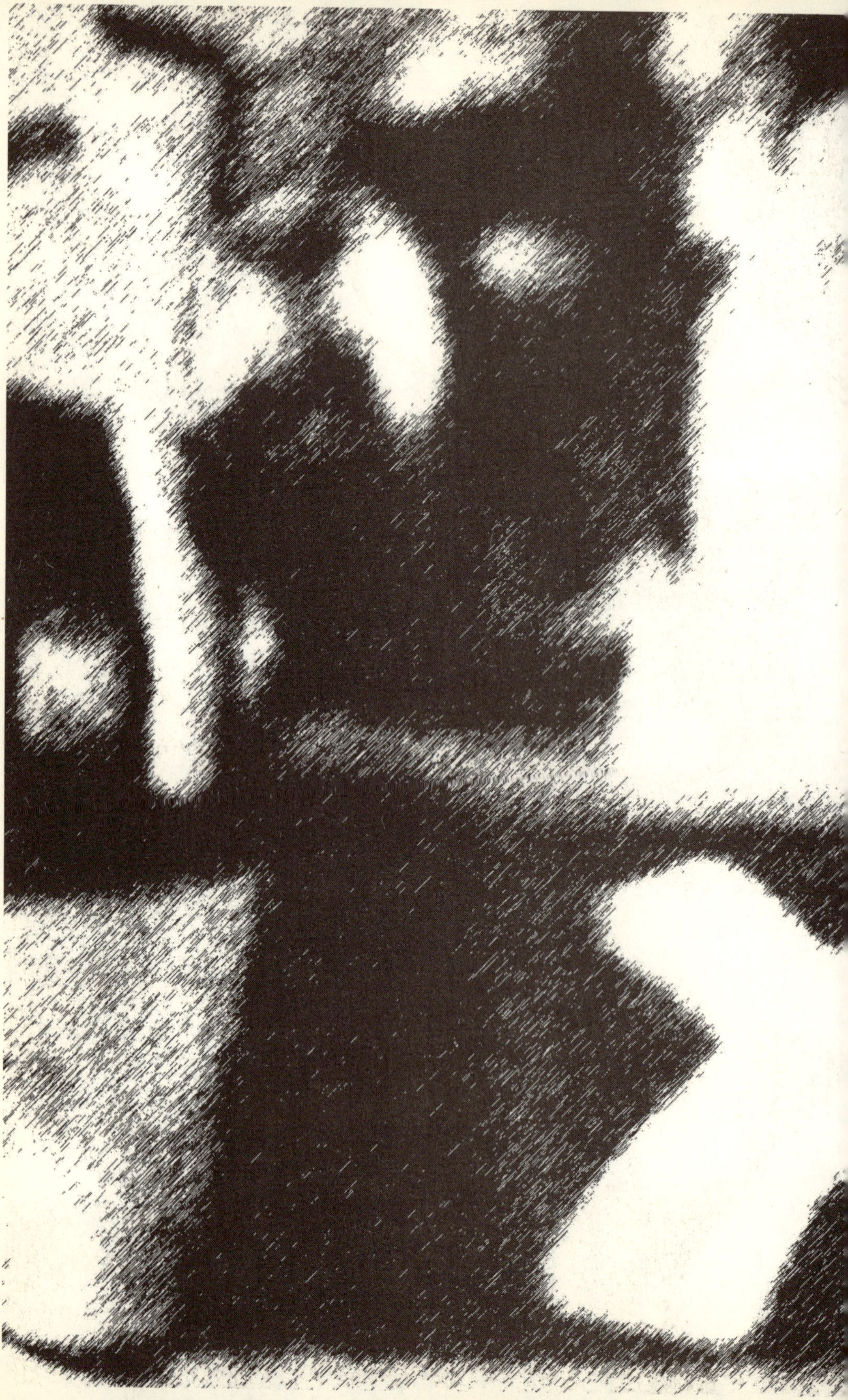

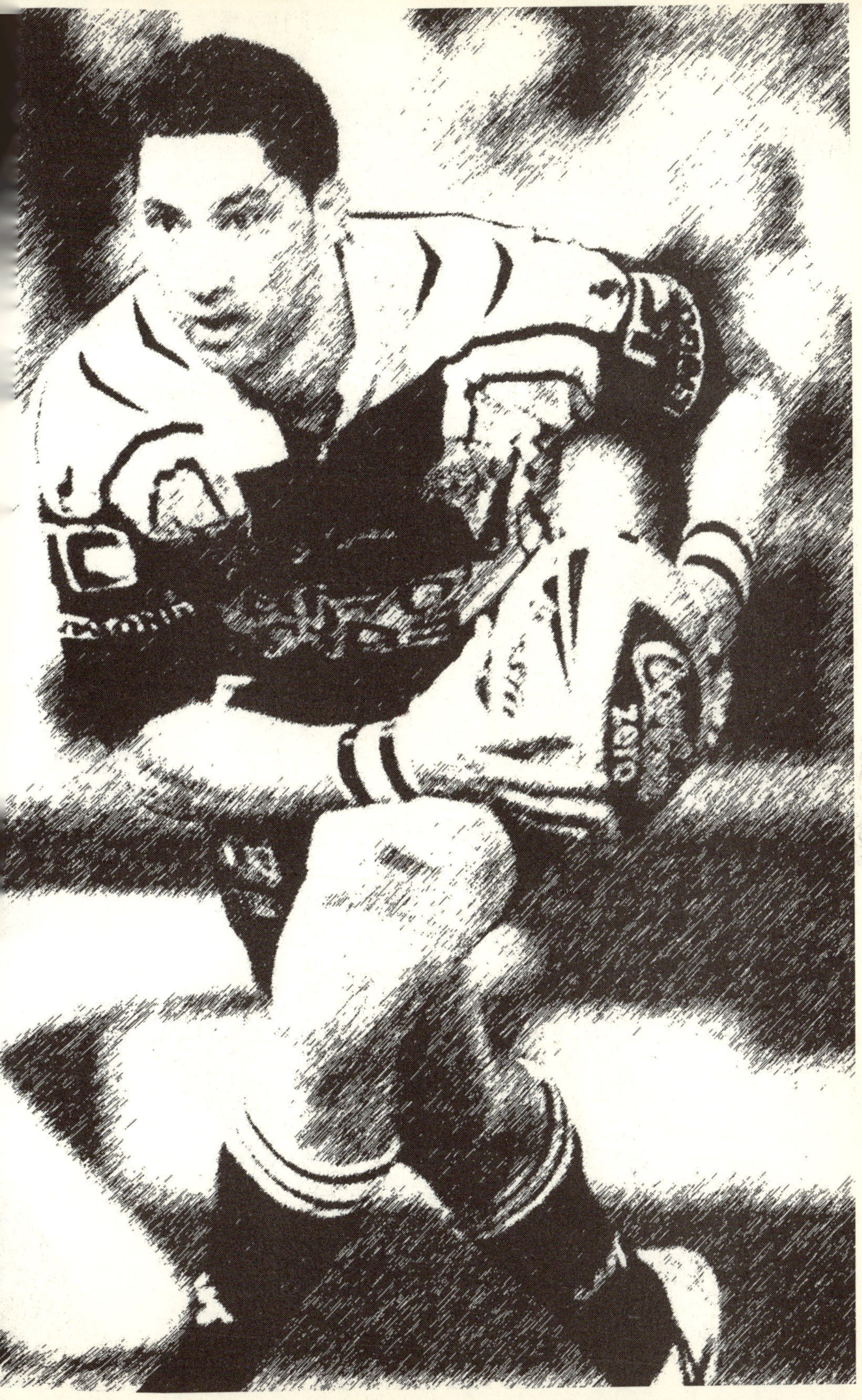